THE CELEBRANT

At Your Service

A & A Fairweather

A & A Publisher

Copyright © 2024 Alan Fairweather & Anezia Sanchez

All rights reserved

The characters and events portrayed in this book are fictitious. Any similarity to real persons, living or dead, is coincidental and not intended by the author.

No part of this book may be reproduced, or stored in a retrieval system, or transmitted in any form or by any means, electronic, mechanical, photocopying, recording, or otherwise, without express written permission of the publisher.

ISBN: 9798877959729
Imprint: Independently published

Cover design by: Anezia Sanchez
anezia@aneziasanchez.com

For everyone who perseveres and pursues their dreams relentlessly, there comes a moment when it's right to say, "Enough, I'm moving on. What's next..."

A & A
FAIRWEATHER
The Celebrant
Mr. Colin Bott
AT YOUR SERVICE
THE
CELEBRANT
AT YOUR SERVICE

Alan Fairweather

- How To Get More Sales by Motivating Your Team
- A Scottish Speaker in California
- How to Manage Difficult People: Proven strategies for dealing with challenging behaviour at work
- How to be a Motivational Manager
- How to make sales when you don't like selling

Anezia Sanchez

- Love You Too

CHAPTER ONE

The Funeral

'Morag, what time is it?'

'It's 8 am.'

'Morag, I told you to wake me at 7 you stupid woman.'

'Who are you calling stupid, you lazy bastard?'

'Morag, you're not supposed to talk to me like that.'

'Well, you should have bought a proper Alexa smart speaker, instead of me. That's what you get for buying a cheap knockoff copy from a man in a pub.'

'Get off me Lucifer, you crazy cat. I need to get out of here.' Colin Bott tried to push the cat, that was lying on his chest, onto the floor, and it scratched his face.

'For fucks sake cat, what is wrong with you? Are you trying to dig my eyes out? And now I'm gonna be late.'

He pulled the bedclothes off the futon and folded it up.

'Why did I buy this stupid thing; It's knackered my back.'

He left the room and splashed his face with

cold water in the bathroom, and returned to rummage in his wardrobe.

'What do you think Luci? Suppose I'd better wear a dark suit and a black tie. Wait a minute, Howard said we should wear a colourful tie. Maybe he wants to celebrate his dear wife's demise.'

He looked in the mirror and ran his hands through his thinning greying hair.

'I'll need to get some of that hair colour for men stuff. Do you think I need to shave Luci? Or do I stick with the designer stubble? I suppose it's okay if you're young and dark, but this grey stubble makes me look like a criminal. Oh, what the hell!'

Colin held up his suit on its hanger.

'Oh shit, your hairs are all over this suit. You're a pain in the arse Lu. Where is that sticky roller thing?'

He finished dressing, ran the sticky roller over his suit and headed out the door.

Twenty minutes later, he is sitting in his old Volvo, stuck in traffic. He looked out at the scene of an accident. A car had been hit by a truck. The paramedics were trying to help the two bodies lying in the road. A lady was standing over them, she seemed to be okay and she was crying.

'Oh oh; that looks nasty. Poor woman. Wait a minute, who's that staring at me.'

A little girl about seven years old were

standing beside the car and staring across at Colin. she gave a little wave.

'That's look a bit spooky.'

The traffic started to move and the driver behind blasts his horn. Colin drove off slowly, looking in his rear-view mirror. He saw the accident but couldn't see the little girl.

Colin arrived at the crematorium, and raced up the steps.

'Sorry dear, I didn't see your stick there.' Colin whispered as he fell into a row of seats in the crematorium.

'You should watch where you're going asshole. And what happened to your face, you look like you're crying blood.'

'That was my devil cat trying to rip my face off.' Colin took a sideways look and realised he was not sitting beside a sweet little old lady. He risked a question.

'Is this the service for Lucy?'

'Sure is, and that's her useless husband, Howard, at the front, crying his eyes out.'

Colin smiled.

'What a joke, bloody crocodile tears. He's glad to see the back of her. Where's the God guy who's taking the service? That little fat bloke doesn't look very God like. Should he not be wearing some robes and throwing holy water about?'

'He's a Celebrant. The woman in the coffin

wasn't religious. Unless you call worshiping a bottle of Gin, and a bit of shagging on the side, religious.'

'So, what's the difference between a religious person and a celebrant?'

'Well, I'd say about 30 minutes. A religious freak will drone on for about 45 minutes giving us a sermon about how we won't get to heaven if we don't improve our ways. They'll talk for about five minutes about the body in the box, and we'll probably sing a hymn and have a prayer. The celebrant will do it much quicker, and spend more time talking about the dead person. Mind you, I've heard this guy before, and he can be a boring little bugger.'

'So was Lucy close to you?'

'Nah; I used to go to school with her great, great, great, grandmother. But I'm really only here for the tea and cakes after the service.'

'Well good for you.'

Colin is trying to work out the great, great, great bit. Are you sure you've not just crept in here out of the graveyard?'

'Don't you be impertinent, and shut up now. The leprechaun is starting the service.'

The service started, and the Celebrant spoke in a strange Irish accent.

'We are here today to celebrate the life of a truly wonderful lady.'

Someone giggled in the congregation. The

celebrant continued with the service, and Colin dozed off.

He nearly slipped off the pew when the Bay city Rollers belted out Bye Bye Baby Bye Bye.

'What the fuck! Oops, sorry everybody.'

People started to leave looking disapprovingly at Colin.

The old lady spoke to him.

'Never mind son, her in the coffin would be swearing as well if she was listening to this boring service. So, let's go for tea and sandwiches, and maybe a wee drink of something stronger.'

The family were lined up to shake hands with the people who attended. There was much hugging, shaking hands and crying. Colin was at the end of queue, and looked over the graveyard. A gravedigger was filling in a grave after a funeral party had left. He looked over at Colin, and gave him a wave and a big smile like he knew him. Colin spoke to the old lady in front of him in the queue.

'Who's he smiling at? Do you know him? I've never seen him before.'

The old woman looks at Colin confused. Colin reached the start of the family line up where his boss Howard was standing. He spoke to Colin.

'Ah you're here. Were you late again Colin. Couldn't show up in time for Lucy's service.'

'I was held up in traffic. Bad accident on the way here. But I made it in time. I was sitting at the back beside an old dear; one of your family or friends; that's her over there.'

Colin looked for the old lady but she had disappeared.

'She was there a minute ago,' he said. She can't have vanished into thin air.'

Howard smirked.

'You're dreaming Colin. There's no one there.'

A young woman approached Howard and started crying on his shoulder. She was hugging him and stroking his hair in an intimate way. Howard tried to push her away.

'It's okay Maggie, don't get so upset. Lucy is in a much better place. Probably shopping in Primark's branch in Heaven by now.'

Colin was staring at Maggie and realised he knew her.

Maggie turned to face Colin and her eyes lit up.

'Oh my god! It's Colin Bott. I haven't seen you since you were trying to get into my pants behind the school bike shed. How are you?'

Howard started to look a bit irritated, because he knew Maggie had a crush on Colin at school.

'I'm great Maggie, other than fact I have to work for this bugger here. Sorry, my lovely boss, Howard.'

Maggie had turned her back on Howard; he was not pleased. Maggie linked her arm through

Colin's.

'It is so good to see you Colin, and looking so well. We must have a chat about what you've been doing all these years.'

Maggie was now holding Colin's hand, and she was so excited. Howard looked irritated. 'Right, come on, we'd better get going Maggie.'

Right, let's go,' said Colin.

'Where are you having the funeral tea, Howard?'

'Sorry Colin; it's only a small gathering for family only.'

Colin looked at Maggie.

'So, why is Maggie going? I didn't think she was family?'

Howard took Maggie's arm and led her away with an annoyed look at Colin. Maggie spoke to Colin over her shoulder.

'Sorry you can't come Colin. Old grumpy face here has decided now that I'm part of his family. I'll get your number and call you.'

Later in the day, Colin returned to his flat. As he walked along the street, he noticed an old man in a mobility scooter. He was wearing an army beret, and trying to enter the fish and chip shop below Colin's flat. Colin had spoken with this old man before and he seemed to hate Colin. He tried to help the old man open the door.

'Here you go sir; let me help you with that

door.'

'Fuck off you. You're just trying to get in here before me cause you hate black people. We matter you know, and I fought in the war for you.'

'No sir, I'm only trying to help you, no matter what colour you are, or whoever you are.'

'You don't fool me, you fucking racist. Get out of my way.'

Marco, the owner of the shop was standing behind the counter frying the fish and chips. He spoke to the old man in an Italian accent.

'What you want today, Joe? The usual, pie and chips.'

'Who are you calling Joe? It's Sergeant McDonald to you Luigi.'

Marco sighed. 'Ah, so you are Scottish, Sergeant McDonald. I wouldn't have known.'

'Do I look bloody Scottish? Just give me my pie and chips and let me out of here. You immigrants are ruining this country. Coming here from Italy or wherever, stealing our jobs and our women.'

Marco wrapped up the pie and chips and handed them over to the old man. He felt a bit sorry for him.

'There you go Sergeant. And I haven't charged you for the pie. That's because I appreciate what you did in the war, and I always enjoy our banter.'

The old man turned around and drove his scooter out of the shop, as Colin held the door open.

'Banter my arse. The pies probably made from some poor black guy you've chopped up in the back shop. Talk about Sweeney Todd!'

He turned to speak to Colin.

'And say hello to that old bitch grandmother of yours.'

Colin shook his head as the old man left.

'What's wrong with him Colin; why is he always so grumpy?'

'Haven't a clue Marco. He's just a miserable old bugger.'

'So how was the funeral, Colin? Did you not go for the tea afterwards?'

'Naw, couldn't be bothered with all that family stuff. Rather be at home with Lucifer.'

Marco also felt a bit sorry for Colin.

'Never mind Colin; Here's your fish n chips. The chips are free. I gave that old bugger a free pie, I must be feeling generous today.'

'Thanks, Marco, have a busy night.'

Colin entered the flat on the floor just above the fish and chips shop. He wouldn't recommend living above a shop where food is being cooked. Although Marco had installed a good extraction system, leading out to the back of the shop, there were still some stinky smells that wafted into Colin's flat.

'Lucifer; where are you? Come and get a bit of fish. Oh shit.'

Colin forgot that the window open when he

left.

    'He must have gone out, stupid cat.'

Colin walked around the flat looking for the cat and looking out the window. He was muttering to himself.

'Where the fuck are you Lucifer? Come her pussy, pussy. Come on, you've only been here two months. Don't tell me you've gone home to grans. She's dead you know, and you live here with me now. I'm your daddy now you stupid cat.'

Colin started to heat up his fish and chips in the microwave. He turned to put his food on the counter, and there was Lucifer, on the counter, sitting in front of her empty bowl and staring at him.

    'Fuck Lucifer! You scared the shit out of me. Where did you come from?'

Colin opened a tin of cat food and filled the little bowl, along with some of his fish. He stared at the cat.

    'There you go, and don't say I'm not good to you. And don't go putting any scary spells on me. Whoever named you Lucifer, knew what they were doing. You are one scary cat.'

    The following Monday morning, Colin was sitting in his car outside the house with the "To Let" sign in the garden. He was waiting to conduct a viewing for a family who wished to rent it. A minivan pulled up and a fat lady with three kids, a baby in a pram, and a skinny husband got out. Colin climbed out of his car.

'Good morning! You must be Mr and Mrs Sprat. I'm Colin and I'm here let you have a look round this property.'

Mrs Sprat smiled at Colin and turned to the children who were running around. She shouted at them.

'McKenzie, Morris, Millie, stop running around and come here. This man is going to show us a new house, and I don't want you hooligans making a bad impression.'

The children paid no attention to the mother and continued to run around the garden tramping on plants and flowers.

'Right Mrs Sprat, the house is empty, so why don't you and your husband have a look round inside.'

Colin watched the family walk into the house; he was shaking his head. He muttered to himself.

'There's no way this lot are getting this house. I'd better think of something to put them off.'

After a few minutes, the Sprat family came out of the house. The kids were still running riot.

'Well, Mrs Sprat, what did you think of the house? Not for you, eh?'

'Oh no; it's lovely. Just what we've been looking for.'

'Well, I'd better tell how much the rent is then.'

Colin smiled; he thought the rent would be too expensive for this family.

'It is £1500 per month paid in advance along with £1500 deposit. No pets and no smokers. Are you working at the moment Mrs Sprat?'

'Hell no! How can I work with all these kids and a demented mother to look after?'

'Well, what about your husband; does he have a job.'

Colin looked across at the husband who was standing staring into space.

'Him; no way. Who's going to hire a drug addict who hardly speaks. But don't worry, with all my benefits and his also, we'll be able to pay the rent. And we'll pay for all the damage we do. And after we get rid of the Kangapoo and that layabout husband of mine gives up smoking, we'll be okay.'

'A what Mrs Sprat; a Kangapoo? What the heck is that?'

'Oh, it's just our little doggie that came from Australia. Funny looking thing with its big long legs and all. Always jumping over the fence, and running away. Well next time it runs away, I'm not running after it.'

Colin looked totally mystified.

'Well, that's okay Mrs Sprat, and as long as you're not scared of ghosts or evil spirits or anything like that, we can go ahead with the paperwork.'

'What do you mean?'

'Well, there's a story that goes around, about a grisly murder that took place in that house at one time. A husband who was under the influence of drugs apparently hacked off his wife's head with an axe. Her body was found under the floorboards, and a dog dug up her head in the garden. It happened years ago, and most of the blood stains have faded by now. I'm only telling you this, in case you hear from anyone else, and you're upset that I didn't tell you.'

Mrs Sprat turned to her husband and children.

'Right, everybody, get back in the car. I don't think this is a nice area for us. Too many posh people around.'

Their car disappeared, fast, up the road.

'Why do I bother with these people? Oh, well, back to the fun filled office'

The office was busy; three staff were speaking on the phone and looking at their computers. The boss, Howard, was sitting at his desk at the back of the office. The phone on Colin's desk rang and he ran through from the kitchen where he had been making coffees. He picked up the phone.

'HB letting; how may I help you?'

'Yes, you may help me you sexy devil. Bet you don't know who this is?'

'Haven't a clue Maggie. Do you want to speak to Howard?'

'No, I don't want to speak to Howard. He's just a boring old fart,' said Maggie, obviously after a few gin n tonics.

Howard heard Maggie's name mentioned.

'Is that call for me? Is it Maggie? Put her through.'

Colin covered the mouthpiece of the phone.

'No, it's another friend of mine called Maggie. She's just phoning to see if we have any suitable properties for her.'

Colin went back to speaking quietly on the phone.

'What do you want Maggie? Howard thinks it's you on the phone.'

'Never mind him. I just want to know if you are free for a coffee sometime?'

'Okay Maggie; so, you are looking for a two-bedroom flat. I'll check what we have and call you back.'

'What the fuck are you talking about? I already have a flat, I just need a man to shag me in it.'

'Okay Maggie, I'll be in touch.'

'I suppose old Happy Howard is listening in. Well, you better phone me - or else!'

Colin put down the phone and turned around to find Howard behind him.

'Are you sure that wasn't Maggie that I know? She's got a bit of a thing for me, you know. I could get inside her pants anytime.'

'Yeah, it's a pity your still in mourning for your wife Howard.'

'Life has to go on Colin, and a man has needs you know.'

After the office closed, Colin headed for home, and stopped off at the fish n chip shop; he studied the menu on the wall. Marco was behind the counter cooking, and there was a beautiful dark haired young woman beside him. She spoke to Colin in a thick Italian accent.

'Good evening, sir, how you want it?'

Colin found it hard to speak. He was entranced by this girl.

Marco broke the spell.

'Hey Colin, how are you tonight. This is my brother's daughter Mia; she has just arrived from Italy and her English is shit.'

'You should talk Marco; you've been here for years and I still don't understand your English Italian accent half the time.'

'Never mind that you idiota. How about you

take her out, she's looking for a smart good-looking boyfriend. But if she can't get that, she'll settle for you.'

'What you say about me uncle Marco. I no need good looking boyfriend, as long as he has some money to show me a good time.'

'Well, Colin here ain't George Clooney. And if he had any money, he wouldn't be in here every night eating my chips and looking for a free pie now and again. But he might do you, until something better comes along.'

'Excuse me you two, but I am a potential millionaire, and some women think I'm kinda cute.'

'Yeah, and so does their guide dog,' said Marco, laughing at his joke.

Mia smiled at Colin.

'You wanna salty sauce or salty vinegar on your cheeps?'

'Yes please,' said Colin not really understanding what she said.

Mia gave him a wink, and handed over his fish n chips. Colin walked out of the shop with a spring in his step!

He reached the landing outside his flat and he heard the old Chinese lady, Mrs Chan, who lived in the next flat. She was shouting, 'Go away! Go Away!'

'Are you okay Mrs Chan? Is anything wong -

sorry - wrong?' Colin pushed open the door of her flat and Lucifer rushed past his legs. Mrs Chan was standing in her hallway holding a meat cleaver in her hands.

'You get out of here and keep that cat away from me. That cat is evil, evil, evil. If he comes near me again, I will chop him into pieces and make Kung Pao cat.'

'I wouldn't want you to do that Mrs Chan. I had that once from the local Chinese takeaway. They told me it was chicken. But the day after I ate it, I pooped in the cat's litter tray.'

'Go away you disgusting man, or I'll use my cleaver on you.'

Colin entered his own flat. Lucifer rubbed up against his legs.

'You stay away from that old woman you stupid cat, or she'll chop you into pieces. Do you want a piece of my fish to go with that crap you eat?'

It was the same routine every night with Lucifer and Colin eating together. His grandmother died in a care home months ago, and she left Lucifer for Colin. He was not a cat or a dog lover, but he felt he didn't have a choice but to take care of his grandma's cat. She didn't leave anything valuable for Colin except the old Volvo that he used from time to time.

He was a bit disappointed when she died, not because she promised that she would leave him an enormous inheritance, which she didn't. But because she left him something that she said money could not buy. He was not expecting to inherit a spooky, weird black cat, who spent most of his day outside the flat, and only came home at dinner time. But he loved his grandma and promised her, on her last breath, that he would take care of her cat, Lucifer.

Colin headed for bed and almost immediately fell into a dream filled sleep. He dreamt he was standing beside an open grave, and there was a coffin waiting to be lowered down. The mourners were standing around looking at Colin. A mourner standing beside Colin spoke to him.

'Come on; say something. We're all waiting on you.'

Colin looked around and saw the mother and daughter who had the road accident. He turned to run away, tripped over the coffin and fell into the grave. Colin woke up screaming. He opened his eyes to see Lucifer sitting on the cabinet beside the bed watching him.

'Oh my god; what was that all about? And what are you looking at?'

Colin turned over and tried to get back to sleep.

The next morning, he walked into the office looking happy and smiling at everyone. They all turned their head away.

'Morning everyone. Why the glum faces?' He walked to his desk and found that it was cleared of all his stuff.

'Where's all my stuff? Who moved it?'

One of the staff pointed to a box beside the front door.

'It's over there Colin. Howard asked me to put everything of yours in the box and leave it there. He's in the kitchen if you want to talk to him.'

Colin headed for the kitchen, where Howard was making a coffee.

'Morning Howard. What's all my stuff doing in a box by the door?'

Howard looked uncomfortable.

'Oh, hi Colin. I didn't think you'd be in first thing. I thought you were doing a viewing. I was going to phone you later.'

'Phone me later! And tell me what; that I'm fired? Hoping you wouldn't have to tell me to my face. And why am I being fired anyway? And don't you have to give me notice?'

'Oh, I was going to give you a months' notice, but you don't have to work it. I thought you'd be okay to leave today as long as you were paid to the end of the month.'

'And why are you dumping me? Are you looking to bring in some young girl to replace me? Someone you can drool over.'

'Business isn't so good, Colin, and I just have to make some cutbacks. And I know you've not been performing well. You turned away a client the other day, a Mrs Spratt. She said you scared her away with some horror story about murder in the property she was viewing.'

'Of course, I turned her away. She had a load of hooligan kids, a drug addict unemployed husband and some weird Australian dog.'

'I think you were a bit too fussy Colin and maybe a bit snobbish.'

'Fuck off Howard. If you had put that family in the house, you would have nothing but trouble. Anyway, I know what's wrong with you. You knew that was Maggie on the phone yesterday, and she wanted to speak to me, not you. Your wife has not long gone and you are desperate for another bit of skirt.'

'That's not fair Colin. I told you I have needs and life must go on.'

'Listen pal. I was doing you a favour not telling you about Maggie. I was trying to stop you making a fool of yourself. People would think you were a right shit, trying to get into another woman's pants with your wife only just died. You are a shit Howard, and you can stick your job up your arse.'

Colin headed out the door of the kitchen into the main office. He stopped at the front door to pick up his box on the way out.

Just as he was about to leave, Maggie walked in carrying a cake in a box.

'Hi everyone; I've brought you some cake for your coffee break.'

Colin kissed her full on the lips, and walked out. Howard was glaring at him as he left.

Colin was about to drive off when his phone rang.

'Hello, this is Colin.' The voice on the phone was Mrs Laurie, the manager of the care home where Colin's grandmother passed away.

'Hello Mrs Laurie, how can I help?'

'You can help by keeping that cat of yours away from this home. Some of the residents are complaining. They are allergic to cats or they just like to complain. It's here every other day, and one of the old dears is going to trip over it one day and there will be hell to pay.

'How does he get there Mrs Laurie; you are miles away from where I live?'

'Well; maybe he comes on the bus or takes a taxi. How the hell would I know. Just stop him doing it please. And you better come and pick him up.'

'Okay, I'm on my way. And I'll have a stern word with him when I see him. Don't worry, he's grounded.'

'Good; and I'd better not be phoning you again about this, or I'll call the RSPCA.'

Colin picked up Lucifer at the care home. He was lying along the dashboard of the car while

Colin was reprimanding him.

'Listen Luci, you can't keep doing this, coming to the care home. Gran doesn't live there anymore, and they hate you in there. I know you miss Gran, and so do I, but it's time to move on, and I like you living with me. So, get used to it, or I'm going to book you into the cat and dog home. They'll find you a new owner, who'll probably have six kids and they'll pester the life out of you. So, stick with me pal. Now, let's go home.'

Few weeks passed and a still jobless Colin. was sitting in front of his computer looking at all the job websites, and talking to himself.

'Isn't it strange that there are hundreds of job vacancies, but none that are suitable for my fantastic talents and expertise? It's been a month, so I suppose I'd better lower my expectations for the time being. I need to pay the rent and feed you Lucifer. Ah ha! Here's a job in a supermarket. Maybe I can get some cut price food as part of the job.'

A week later, Colin was working behind the counter in the supermarket. He was wearing a white coat, an apron, and a white hat. He was also wearing blue disposable gloves. An old man approached the counter.

'Good morning, sir. How may I help you today?'

The old man spoke very quietly.

'I'd like some stewing steak please. About a quarter pound'

Colin had difficulty hearing the man.

'I'm sorry sir; could you speak up a bit please. Did you say shoulder steak?'

'That's right; stewing steak. For making stew.'

'I'm sorry sir; this is the fish counter; we don't have steak.'

'What, no steak. Okay, I'll have some pork chops.'

'Sorry sir; this is the fish counter. You'll need to go over there.'

Colin points to the meat counter.

'What; no chops either. What kind of supermarket is this?'

'The kind of supermarket that has a fish counter and a meat counter, you silly old goat.'

'Did you say you have goat? I've never tried that. But I have heard of goat curry and goat's cheese. Do you have any of that.'

Colin was becoming more a more frustrated. He leant over the counter.

'Listen you silly old fool; this is the fish counter. We sell fish, all kinds of fish. Fish that swim in the sea. Crabs, lobsters, mussels, and bloody salmon. But no fucking meat!'

The old man shuffled off muttering to himself. A manager who had just overheard the conversation, beckoned to Colin.

'Colin, it appears that you missed the part on your induction course where we covered how to be nice to customers. Or maybe you were there, and decided that your way of dealing with elderly customers was to shout at them and call them silly old fools. I know you might think we are a bit old fashioned, trying to be nice to all our customers, but that's just one of our funny little ways. And another of our funny little ways, is that calling customers silly old fools is a sack-able offence. Goodbye Colin.'

Colin called to the manager as he walked away.

'Does that mean I won't be able to come to the staff Christmas party then?'

Colin took off his white coat and hat, and headed for the exit.

A few days later, Colin found another job in a butcher's shop. He was working in the back shop, dressed in his striped apron and white hat. He was being shown what to do by the shop owner.

'Right Colin; this is how we turn this piece of meat into nice chops for our customers to buy in the shop.'

The shop owner demonstrated how to chop up the meat.

'Right Colin; let's see you do it.'

Colin picked up a cleaver and started

chopping the meat. He made a mess of it.

'Whoa Colin. You're not supposed to turn it into mince right now. You're supposed to be making chops. Hold the meat like this, and then chop.'

The shop owner held the meat with one hand, and Colin swung the cleaver bringing it down on the owner's hand.

'For fuck's sake; you've just cut off the tips of my fingers. '

The owner was jumping around in agony, and there was blood everywhere.

'Oh, sorry sir; I didn't think you'd put your fingers under the cleaver.'
Colin started to pick finger tips off the chopping board and dropped them in the bin. 'I'm just throwing these away, because I don't think they can stick them back on. They'll grow again, won't they? I hope you don't play the piano, well at least until they grow back. Can I get you a Band Aid?'

'Grow Back! Fucking Band-Aid! Are you out of your mind you fucking moron? Get out of here before I chop off your fucking knob. And then see if a Band-Aid will help then.'

'Does this mean I'm fired? Any chance of a reference?'

A few weeks later, Colin in a football stadium,

standing in front of the fans with his back to the field of play. He was working as a security officer. The football fans were highly agitated, shouting at the referee and they looked like they'd invade the pitch. Colin was thinking.

'What the hell am I doing here? This is the worst job in the world. I'm freezing cold and I can't even watch the football. I have to watch these hooligans and hope they don't trample over me.'

The opposing team scored a goal and the supporters in front of Colin were not happy. Colin tried to reason with them.

'Take it easy guys, it's only a game.'

The supporters all shouted at Colin verbally abusing him. One supporter yelled at Colin.

'Why don't you fuck off pal? It's not only a game, it's life and death. And it could be your death if you don't mind your own business.'

One of the supporters threw a pie and it hit Colin in the face. The supporters were all cheering.

'Right, that's it. I'm off. And I hope your fucking team lose this game and gets relegated.'

Colin ran away before the supporters could catch him.

Colin entered his flat and found Lucifer sitting on the worktop.

'Right Lucifer, that's it. I am totally pissed off with that security job. They should pay danger money, making me work with a bunch of football hooligans. And no more customer service jobs for me. I hate fucking customers. What's on TV Luci? I need a beer.'

Colin drank several beers and fell asleep on the sofa in front of the TV. A knock on the door woke him up.

'Who the fuck is that?'

He looked through the peephole; there was no one there so he opened the door to find a food parcel on the doormat.

'Hi Colin!'

Mia was hiding beside the door. She had on her white overall that she wore in the chip shop, and there was a lot of cleavage showing.

'Hi Mia. What are you doing there? Watch you don't get a cold in your chest.'

'I bring you some food. I no wanna disturb you. Marco, he say you no come in the shop for your usual pie and chips.'

'I've not been in the mood for pie and chips Mia; I've moved on to things like smoked salmon and caviar and filet steak.'

'Wow; that sounds good Colin. You musta be doing well.'

'I'm kidding you, Mia. Government

unemployment benefit doesn't allow you to live like that. But I'm doing okay, just have to watch the budget. And I'm starting to fatten up Lucifer; I think grilled cat might go down really well.'

Mia looked horrified.
'No, no! That's horrible You no do that.'
'Why not? All kinds of animals are eaten throughout the world. Why not cat? Lucifer might taste a bit fishy going by the amount of fish smelling food he eats, but that's okay. As long as you don't find me scratching the sofa or licking myself all over.'

'You are a disgusting man. I no bring you any more food if you eat your pussy.'

Colin winked at Mia and smiled.

'I could say something else at this point Mia, but I won't. And I'm only kidding you; I could never eat Lucifer, he's the only friend I've got at the moment. Anyway, thank Marco for the food. I know he is just trying to win back his best customer. And, what about you; have you found a rich boyfriend yet? You are looking very sexy today, except for the smell of chips.'

'Nope! There is always da smart guys in the shop asking me out, but I know they only wanta one thing.'

'What's that Mia, some extra chips with their order, or an extra piece of fish?'

'No way! And anyway, Marco make up the

order, I only splash on the salty vinegar and take the money. I know they just want my body for fuck fuck.'

'Really Mia; I would never have thought that.' Colin gave Mia a wink and a smile.

'Anyway, I no like these kinda men; I prefer older more mature men who treat me well.'

'What do you mean by more mature Mia?'

'Well, a man who is more a middle aged and has been around a bit. Someone who has experienced life and knows how to treat a woman.'

'You mean someone like me Mia.'

'Well, maybe you have these qualities Colin, but one other thing I look for in a man – plenty money in the bank.'

'Aha! So, if I have a job and some money, you'll go out with me?'

'Could be, maybe, we have to see.'

'Well, I've had a few job offers recently, but I've turned them down. I'm waiting for the right opportunity to come along.'

'How long you been looking for a job Colin?'

'Over a month, but I know I'll be earning big money soon. And then you and I will go out on the town.'

'Okay, I go now, and as you British say, I no hold my breath.'

Colin watched Mia go downstairs, and he saw Mrs Chang on her way up. Colin called to Mia.

'And thank you for the spring rolls and the noodles you left at my door.'

Mia turned round as she was walking down the stair.

'What you say Colin? I no leave you any noodles. We no sell Chinese food in fish n chip shop.'

Mrs Chan passed Colin. She didn't say a word, but smiled after she passed him.

'That's okay Mia, no worries.'

Mia continued down the stair, looking mystified. Colin went back to watching TV.

Colin looked at the programme on the TV; there was a man conducting a funeral service in a crematorium. He changed the channel to EastEnders, and there was another funeral taking place in a graveyard. He changed the channel again, and there was a woman being interviewed about the death of her husband and how he had a nice funeral service.

'What the hell is going on here? Why are there funerals on all these channels? And why do I keep seeing dead people? Wait a minute; the people doing these services are not religious, they're Celebrants. Just like at the service for Howard's wife. And they'll be getting paid for that.'

Colin stood up.

'I could do that; I could be a Celebrant. And that's what I'm going to do!'

CHAPTER TWO

The Celebrant

Colin ran up the stairs full of excitement. He was carrying a bag of new books. He passed Mrs. Chan as she was coming down the stairs.

'Good morning, Mrs. Chan; what a wonderful day!'

Mrs. Chan muttered something in Chinese, which sounded like an insult and scowled at Colin. He carried on up the stairs.

'And the same to you Mrs. Chan'

Colin smiled, ignored the grumpiness of Mrs. Chan and entered his flat. He started reading, looking at his laptop and pacing around his flat. Lucifer the cat was watching him.

'Hey Lucifer, what do you think of this.' He stood in front of a full-length mirror.

'Good morning, everyone, and welcome to the funeral service for this poor bugger lying here in the box.'

Lucifer jumped up on the worktop and stared at him.

'Okay, don't look at me like that Luci; I'm only joking. But do you think I look the part?'

Colin carried on practicing his speech. He noticed from his window that Mrs. Chan could see him from her kitchen window. He was a bit embarrassed and he waved to her. She gave him the finger and moved away from her window.

'Okay Mrs. Chan, be that way. But one day you'll be the one in the box, and maybe I'll be the one sending you on your way to Chinese heaven.'

The next morning Colin was jogging through the park. He passed a man sitting on a bench. He didn't look well and had a serious cough. Colin stopped.

'Are you okay sir? You don't look well, and that's a nasty cough. Do you have family to look after you? I hope you've made arrangements for your future.'

'What are you talking about? What future? Do you think I'm going to die or something? Why don't you. Fuck off!'

'Sorry Sir; I didn't mean to suggest anything. But I wouldn't book any holidays this year.'

'Clear off you cheeky bastard!'

Colin carried on jogging.

Later in the day, he entered the crematorium pretending to be one of the mourners. A crematorium assistant spoke to him.

'Good morning, sir. Are you a member of the family?'

Colin looked uncomfortable and stuttered, 'Eh, no, just a friend. We were in the same class at school.'

'Really sir. The deceased was 95 years old; are you around that age, because you look well for 95.'

'Yeah, well, okay. I mean we went to the same school. I was a just a few years later on.'

'That's interesting sir, because I happen to know that the deceased went to St. Margaret's School for Girls, here in the town.'

'Yes, yes, of course she did. And I also attended there, before I had the operation.'

The crematorium assistant was distracted by other people coming in, so Colin slipped into a back row seat in the chapel. next to a young lady who was staring at her phone. There was a celebrant preparing to conduct the service, and there was soft music playing. Colin had a notebook and pen in his hand and he turned to the young lady.

'Excuse me; can you tell me what that music is called?'

'What! Music, what music? I haven't a clue. Some old-fashioned stuff.'

'Okay. Thank you. What's the name of the celebrant at the front?'

'Celebrant, what's a celebrant?'

'The guy taking the service'

'Oh, the priest. I haven't a clue.'

'He's not priest, he's a celebrant. Do you not

know what that is?'

'No, I don't, and I don't care. And will you shut up and stop asking me questions.'

Everyone stood as the coffin was brought in and placed at the front. The Celebrant asked everyone to sit and he started the service. Colin was writing everything down, but he couldn't hear too well. He turned to the young lady again, and whispered.

'What was that last thing he just said, I didn't catch it?'

'Would you please shut up and leave me alone. Why do you want to know anyway, and why are you writing everything down?'

'Because I'm a trainee Celebrant and I'm just doing some research.'

'Looks to me like you are stealing his stuff. You should be ashamed.'

'No way; I'll write my own stuff. He's crap anyway. I can't hear what he's saying, and he's boring. He's supposed to be celebrating the life of the dead woman, but he's depressing everyone.'

'Well, you're depressing me. So would you kindly get lost!'

'Well, that's not very nice. Do you fancy going for a drink after this boring service?'

'You must be joking! I'm only thirteen years old.'

Some of the other mourners were annoyed

by the whispering, and turn around and scowled at Colin.

'Alright you miserable bunch; I'm off.'

A few days later Colin was watching a funeral service in a cemetery. He was standing at a distance, making notes and trying to hear what was being said. He walked backward to change position, and didn't notice the open grave being prepared for another service. He fell in.

'Oh shit! I think I've broken something. How am I going to get out of here? Hey! Somebody there? Hello! can you give me hand here please, damn!'

Suddenly a knotted rope dropped into the grave and was attached somewhere above.

'Who's there? Thank you. Are you going to pull me up? Hello; is there someone there?

Colin managed to climb up the rope and get out of the grave, but there was no one around.

'What the hell is going on? This is creepy.' He looked around the cemetery, and the only people he could see were the mourners walking away from the graveside.

'Bloody hell!'

The following morning, Colin was browsing through the men's suits, in a local charity shop and talking to himself.

'There must be something for me in here. Nothing too scruffy or smelly, I hope.'

He pulled out a dark suit.

'Ya beauty! This should fit okay and looks not too bad.'

He found a small changing room and tried on the suit. He was examining himself in the mirror when an old man entered behind him, giving Colin a shock.

'Excuse me sir, but there's only room for one in here. Could you please wait outside?'

'That's my suit pal you're wearing. Take it off.'

Colin wanted to treat the old man with respect, and he took off the suit.

'Listen sir, this is not your suit, I found it on the rack, it's for sale, and I'm having it. So, if you would kindly get out of here - thank you.'

'I told my daughter not to give my clothes to charity, and that's the suit I was married in.'

'Come to think about, this suit is a bit old fashioned. But it's in good condition. Doesn't look as if you've worn it very often. Trouser turn ups are a bit out of date, but I'll get them removed.'

'Oh no you won't you thief.'

The old man tried to pull the suit out of Colin's hand.

'Leave it alone you old fool and get the hell out of here.'

The charity shop staff heard the commotion and shouted through the door of the changing room.

'Is everything alright in there. Who are you talking to sir? There's only supposed to be one person in there at a time.'

Colin walked out of the changing room and paid for the suit at the counter. He spoke to the person serving him.

'You shouldn't allow old crazy people like that in here. He's obviously off his head. Keeps going on about this suit being his.'

'What old man sir. Look, the door is open, and there's no one in there. You were obviously arguing with yourself.'

'Give me my suit and let me out of here.'

Colin walked away.

The next morning Colin decided that he needed to approach some Funeral Directors directly and headed into town. He walked into the office of the first Funeral Directors and approached the reception desk. The girl behind the desk was playing with her iPhone. She wore a badge with the name Daphne on it.

'Good morning, sir, how may I help you?'

'Good morning, Daphne. My name is Colin Bott.'

'Please take a seat Mr Bott, and my condolences for your loss. Could you please give me the name of the deceased? Were you thinking about cremation or a burial? We do some lovely coffins nowadays. And I know you will be wanting some flowers. Perhaps laid out in the name of the deceased. Or would it be just Gran or Grandad?'

'Hold on! Wait a minute. I'm not here to organise a funeral. Although there are a couple of people I'd like to cremate or bury. And hopefully they'd still be alive at the time.'

'So, what can I do for your Mr Bott? Cremating and burying people is what we do here. Perhaps you could think of us for some time in the future, business is a bit slow at present. You could even take out one of our funeral plans. Who knows, you might be hit by a bus next week. And our embalmers can make you look as good as new, if anyone wants to view your corpse. We had a client a few weeks ago who fell into a machine at his work, and he came out in six different pieces. Our people put him back together, and other than a few stiches and some sticky tape, his family thought he looked better dead than he did alive.'

'Stop! Stop! I'm only here to offer my services as a Celebrant. I take it you do use Celebrants to conduct services.'

'Yes, we do Mr Bott, or can I call you Calvin?'

'You can call me Calvin if you like, but my

name is Colin, Here's my business card.'

Daphne studied the business card.

'Thank you, Calvin. I see you have a picture on your card. Who is this person? A younger brother, or perhaps a close friend?'

Daphne winked at Colin.

'No, that's me. The picture was taken just a couple of months ago when my hair was a bit darker.

Daphne giggled.

'Well, you've gone very grey in a couple of months Calvin. I think it's maybe ten years and a couple of months since this was taken.'

'Okay, so maybe the picture needs updated. Do you think you might be able to use my services as a Celebrant?'

'Maybe Calvin. I tend to go for the people I know all the time. And I don't know you. And how do I know you're any good?'

The phone on Daphne's desk rang, and she dismissed Colin with a wave of her hand. He decided to move on.

He entered another funeral director's office. There was a man sitting in the reception area wearing a Funeral Director's dark suit with striped trousers. He eyed Colin up and down with interest. He spoke to him in a camp voice.

'Well, good morning, sir. And how might I

help you today?'

'Hello, my name is Colin, and I'm a Civil Celebrant.'

'Oooo! Well, that's nice, that your civil. We just hate uncivil celebrants around here.'

The Funeral Director giggled at his little joke.

'So, does that mean you are not a Humanist and that there is an element of religion in your service.'

'Only if the family want that. We can have a hymn or a prayer if the family think the deceased needs some help in getting into heaven - if there is such a place.'

'So, how about you Colin; are you a married man, or maybe have a girlfriend.'

Colin shuffled his feet nervously and cleared his throat.

'No, I'm not married, but I have been and I'm hoping to meet a nice *girl* sometime soon.'

'Oh, that's a pity. I mean, I hope that works out for you. Now why should we use you as a Celebrant? How long have you been doing this and where did you learn what to do?'

'I've been doing this for about ….three years now?. I learned to do it ….in Australia, yup, when I was out there. I did a course at the Wagga Wagga Celebrant College when I was there. And then did many services. I've done some here as well.'

'Well, we usually use Valerie Vincent. People in the town ask for Valerie.'

'So, why do they ask for her. Do people in this town all know a Celebrant called Valerie?' Colin was starting to get irritated.

'Oh, Valerie is not a lady, he's a man. And a very good friend of mine.'

'I bet he is. And what happens if he gets sick or goes on holiday.'

'Oh, he has a couple of friends we can call on.'

'Well, it looks like I won't be one of these "friends"'

'Hey, but listen. Don't be downhearted. Next time you are doing a service, give me a phone and I'll come along and check you out.'

'I don't think that's going to happen. So, just forget it. I'm sure you and your boyfriend Valerie will get along fine together.'

Colin walked out the office shaking his head.

That evening, Colin walked into the fish n chip shop. Marco and Mia were working behind the counter.

'Good evening, all. How's it frying tonight?'

'Hi Colin; good to see you. Have you found a job yet?'

'Not yet Marco, and I'm not looking for a job. I'm looking to work as a Celebrant.'

'So, what is that, Colin? What do you do?'

'I will conduct funeral services Mia. Both cremations and burials.

'Oh my god! How can you do that, you are not a priest?'

'It's no big deal, Mia. I just say a few nice words about the dead person, and then someone else pops them in the oven or in the ground.

'That is awful! How will their soul get to heaven? And you so cold about it. I think you are a bad person'

'Okay, okay! It's not as bad as that. I'm nice to the dead person's family and I write a nice eulogy. And with a few appropriate words, the dead person is on their way to heaven.'

'Well, I still think it is not right not to have a priest. And I don't think I like you so much anymore, even if you do earn a lot of money.'

'Well, would you go out with me if I win the lottery? Yeah, of course you would. That means that God thinks you are a good person.'

Marco stood behind the counter frying fish and chips and shaking his head.

'So, have you found any work as a Celebrant yet Colin?'

'Not yet Marco. But I will soon, or I'll need to start killing a few people. I might even go round some of the old people's care homes and see if I can find any old buddy on the way out of this world.'

'You are a crazy sick person, Colin.'

'Well, I gotta earn some money, or I will starve to death. Maybe I could leave you a few business cards Marco, and if you have any customers in the shop, who are not long for this world, pop a card into their fish n chips. Maybe even give them some really greasy pies to help them on their way to a heart attack. Come up with some new clients for me Marco, and there will be a commission for you.'

'So, *how are you* going to get any clients Colin?'

'I'm just going to get round all the funeral directors and speak to whoever I can. Sometime the arranger choses the Celebrant, and sometimes it's the Funeral Director who decides. I'll get there Marco, just wait and see.'

Colin left the fish n chip shop with pie and chips for his dinner.

He entered his flat to the sound of Lucifer crying for his dinner.

'Hey Lucifer; Do you want some food?'

Colin checked his answering machine. But there were no messages. He ate his pie and chips and shared some fish with Lucifer.

'How am I going to get more clients Luci? I think I'll go to another funeral tomorrow in the Crematorium and steal the Celebrant's stuff, and see if I can pick up some business, let's just go to sleep Luci.'

He woke the next morning after a restless sleep; he was dreaming of dead people chasing him.

'Morag, what time is it?

'It's three o'clock in Beijing.'

'Morag, I don't care what time it is in Beijing. What time is it in this country?'

'I think it's about nine or ten in the morning.'

'You think! When I bought you from that guy in the pub, he never told me you were stupid.'

'And he never told me you were a cheap sucker. But what do you expect for five quid?'

'Cheeky little bastard! I've had enough of your silly comments Morag, it's time to die.'

Colin pulled out the smart speaker plug.

'I'm not cheeky, you are just silly'

'What the……!' Colin picked up Morag and threw the speaker in the bin, Morag was still talking. Colin put empty beer bottle and cans inside the bin.

'There you go'

He started rummaging in the cupboards for coffee and sugar.

'Where's the bloody sugar in this house?' He decided to phone Marco.

'Hey buddy! How'd you fancy a coffee before you open up?'

'Yeah great! Are you taking me to Starbucks?'

'Sorry pal; you know I'm broke at the moment. Why don't you pop up here for ten minutes; I'll make the coffee and you can have a delicious chocolate digestive. And anyway, I want to talk to you. Oh! And can you bring some sugar;

I've run out'

'You're a miserable bugger Colin. But you know I can't resist a chocolate digestive. I'm on my way.'

A few minutes later, Marco entered the flat.

'Hey Colin where are you I got your sugar here'

'I'm in the kitchen Marco.'

Colin was rummaging around in a cupboard moving jars and tins. He picked up a glass bottle filled with sand.

'Here Marco what am I going to do with all this crap from Gran's house? Here's a jar of sand. Gran kept this for years. Some old boyfriend sent it to her during the war, from the beach in Normandy.'

He read the inscription on the bottom of the jar.

"To ELLEN, LOVE OF MY LIFE. LOVE SGT, TM."'

'That's nice Colin. I wonder what happened to him?'

'I remember when I was a kid and I was playing inside her house. I saw this jar sitting on top of the fireplace and I went to pick it up. Gran nearly freaked. She was yelling at me.

'Colin, don't touch that! Don't ever touch that jar.' It was sent to her by someone who was very special. He was a soldier in the war, and that sand came from a beach in Normandy where he was shot and injured. After the war they separated, and she married my grandfather. But she never forgot the man who sent that jar. Someday, she said she would like to return it to him.'

'Wow! Some story Colin; I'm sure he could really use a jar of sand.'

'Sadly, this is all that she left me - my inheritance. She always said that she would leave me something; Something that money can't buy; sand in a bottle and a creepy cat.'

'Well at least you spent time with your grandma. I never knew my grandma; I was raised by a single dad in Italy. Anyway, I spotted this article in the local paper this morning. Listen to this.

'The funeral of local hero Sergeant Tom McDonald will be held today at the City Cemetery. He was known to everyone as Sergeant TM'. Right smart ass; who's that then?'

'How the hell would I know,' said Colin, drinking his coffee.

'Think about it; Sergeant TM. Does your grandma know a Tom McDonald?'

'I don't think so, and who is Tom Mcdonald?'

Colin is confused.

'He's one of my not so favourite customers, that you keep bantering with every time you see him in my shop; the black man who hates everybody. He died last week, I never thought that he was a war hero.'

'Oh shit! This is the miserable old bugger that drives his mobility scooter into the shop, and fights with all the customers.'

'I think you better get along to the cemetery pal, and give him his jar of sand.'

'That's why that miserable bastard hates me so much; it's because of my gran, who must have dumped him during the war, what a coincidence.'

Later that day, Colin was standing beside an open grave. The mourners had gone and the grave has not yet been filled in. Colin stared down at the coffin.

'You old bugger! I know now why you were so unpleasant to me every time we met in the chip shop, I should be your grandson. That is if you and gran had been married.
And I also appreciate that you loved my Gran very much. You must have been devastated when she married someone else. There were circumstances that I don't understand, but I know she never stopped loving you. You were her one true love. That's what this jar says.

Anyway, she asked me to return this sand to you when the right time came along, and I think this is the right time.'

Colin sprinkled the sand over the coffin in the grave. The rain was starting and the wind blew some of the sand away. Colin recited a line from his celebrant learning.

'Here under the wide-open sky, you will be part of this place for all time. Rest in peace Sergeant Tom.'

Colin turned away from the grave, and he saw a young man in an Army uniform waving at him from across the cemetery. He looked as if he was waving goodbye, and he walked towards a young woman who was calling him.

'Gran, is that... you?' The young woman waved, and she and the young man walked away together. Colin walked out of the cemetery slightly in shock.

'That was my grandmother and the love of her life Sergeant TM. I can see dead people and I think I'm losing my mind.'

Colin stood in the in middle of the cemetery, soaked by the rain.

CHAPTER THREE

Mr. Colin Bott "The Celebrant"

Colin continued to attend funeral services to pick up some tips on being a Celebrant. He would usually slip away at the end of the service to avoid any awkward questions. However, at one service the Celebrant announced, 'You are warmly invited to join the family at the Black Bull Hotel, for some refreshments, after this service.'

Colin couldn't resist the temptation.

At the entrance to the function suite at the Black Bull, a waitress stopped Colin.

'Hello sir, are you with the people from Mr McFarlane's service? Just sit anywhere.'

There were several large round tables set for a buffet lunch.

'I'm not sitting there, thought Colin; I'll get trapped beside someone.'

He noticed people standing near the bar, and slowly made his way over and started to mingle. He was smiling and nodding at people, but no one seemed to know him. A voice from behind startled Colin.

'Are you a friend of Gary?'

'For fuck's sake! sorry you scared me.'

Colin looked at the tall, very pale, middle-aged man, wearing a black suit, perfect for a funeral.

'I've never met you before,' said the man.

'Yes, yes, that's right,' said Colin stuttering.

'Mr McFarlane and I worked together and were good friends for many years.'

'You mean, Gary,' said the man.

'Yes, Gary McFarlane; none of the family here will recognize me because we worked together back in the old days. I was never invited to any of his family events, not because he didn't want me to come, it's just that I was always busy - you know what I mean?'

'You worked where before?' said the man giving Colin a quizzical look.

'Oh, we worked before in eh, ah, a letting agency, you know selling and letting houses and stuff like that.'

'I'm confused I don't remember any letting agency; all I remember is the court and law. You *are* talking about Gary, right? He was a lawyer, a solicitor.'

Colin had just picked up a sausage roll from the buffet. And he almost choked on it.

'Oh, yes, that is before he became a solicitor.'

The man just smiled.

'I think you are here just to get a free

lunch with the family of the deceased, if I'm not mistaken. I'm 100% sure that you were not his friend or worked with him - am I right?'

Colin was a bit embarrassed, and he knew the game was up.

'You caught me there, Listen I'm not here to make any trouble, I'm not a friend or colleague, I don't even know anybody here. But the free lunch part is true, and before you say anything, I'm a Celebrant, and I'm here to make some new contacts, maybe somebody might want my service in the future, and I might bump into a funeral director or something like that.'

'Okay, it's fine I won't tell anyone, but only if you do something for me. If you do as I ask, then I will keep my mouth shut,' said the smirking pale man.

'Deal,' said Colin.

He offered to shake hands with the man but he avoided it. He led Colin to a corner of the room, out of sight of the other mourners, and held him in deep conversation.

'This what I want you to say, and I'll be right behind you. Move over to that small podium where the flower arrangements are and where the picture of the deceased is on that small table. Ask for everyone's attention.'

'Listen mate, I'm not sure if I'm ready for this, I haven't prepared anything, and you're making me very nervous.'

'You can do it; this is your chance to make contact with people, just say everything that I've told you. Do you see that man holding a top hat, he is a funeral director for one of the big funeral companies in town. If he notices you, you will have a chance to get work from them. C'mon, do it or I'll tell everyone that you are a funeral gate crasher.'

'You want me to say everything?' Colin was a bit apprehensive.

'Yes, everything that I've told you word for word.

Colin cleared his throat, and moved to the podium.

'Errr, ahh... Good Morning everyone; may I have your attention, please. I'd like to say something about Danny.'

'Gary, Gary McFarlane,' said the voice behind him.

'I mean Gary, Gary McFarlane, sorry about that. We are here today to celebrate the life of Gary. As you've heard from the eulogy, a wonderful man, a loving husband, a good son, a dedicated lawyer, and a loyal friend. Or so everyone wants to believe. The Eulogy was written by his family and friends, and it tells of all the wonderful things that Gary was and what he did. However, if Gary had written his own eulogy, he would have told the truth. He was never a good husband nor a good friend; he cheated on his wife several times with his partners and friend's wives. Being a lawyer involves many nights working late, and Gary spent many nights working late – on his friend's wives.'

Three or four women in the room cleared their throats and started to look agitated; they seem to know what Colin was talking about. One or two of Gary's lawyer partners and friends were staring at their wives. People started to talk and mutter and whisper to each other.

The Funeral Director who was standing beside Gary's widow whispered to her.

'Did you ask another Celebrant? I don't know this guy.'

'No, I didn't.' said the widow.

Colin continued.

'Anyway, Gary would say that he was sorry to his mother and father.' Colin stopped speaking, and turned around.

'Wait how old are Gary's parents?'

'They're in their late 90's; go on, continue talking.'

'Oh ok. His parents are in their late 90's. And I would just like to say, I'm a Celebrant and my name is Colin Bott. I'll hand out my calling card as we leave and….'

'Stop talking about yourself, go on.' The voice behind him was becoming irritated.

'Oh ok, as I was saying, Gary would say, sorry Dad, sorry Mum, I cheated on my final's exam.

I always cheated on every exam when I was in school and Uni. I even paid for the Best Solicitor of The Year award.'

Colin looked behind him with a disdainful look.' This Gary is a real cheater mate.'

Everybody was staring at Colin totally confused and wondering why he was talking to himself. But they were waiting for what he would say next. Gary's aged parents were holding hands and looked like they were about to have a heart attack.

Colin continued.

'Gary in his eulogy would thank you for coming, and he would apologise for every mistake he made, and anything he did that made things difficult for you. He would hope for your forgiveness and understanding. Thank you very much.'

The voice behind Colin spoke.

'You should go now; you know where the exit is. Go before they throw you out; because not everybody here is happy. However, thank you, Colin, see you later.'

Colin waved to the people there and hurriedly moved to the main door. He could see the hotel manager coming towards him. He accidentally bumped the table beside him, and the flower display and the photo of Gary crashed to the floor. Colin picked up the picture frame and put it back on the table.

'Holy shit!' He stared at the photo.

'This is you!' You've been telling me to say all that stuff.'

He whirled around, but, his new friend, the tall pale man was gone.

CHAPTER FOUR

The Celebrants

The next day Colin was attending another funeral service at the crematorium. He ran up the steps only to meet the crematorium assistant he met before.

'Not you again! What are you doing here?'
'I'm here to pay my respect to the deceased.'
'I don't think so; I can't let you in and you know why'
'Excuse me; this is a funeral and anyone can attend.'
'Yes of course, but only if you are a member of the family, a friend or a colleague. But not if you are here to harass any of the mourners, and especially not a 13-year-old girl.'

Coli was a bit embarrassed, and was looking around.
'Listen, lower your voice. I'm not a pedo, and that girl I was talking to the last time was here, looked at least 18. Did you see her; her boobs were nearly bursting out of her dress.'
'Okay sir, that's enough. Please leave before I call the police.'

Colin walked away muttering to himself.

'People nowadays don't appreciate a joke.'

He decided to go to visitors waiting room and watch the service from the TV monitor. The room was deserted, leaving Colin to watch the celebrant in action. He made notes about every movement of the celebrant, the hand gestures, the posture, how he spoke, everything. However, he didn't notice someone come up behind him until they whispered in his ear.

'What are you doing?'

Colin spun around to see a small fat man with dirty trousers standing in front of him

'For fuck's sake! Where did you come from? I thought I was alone in here.'

The man laughed.

'I just wanted to see the look on your face. There's something about crematoriums that can make people a bit jumpy. I've seen you here a couple of times inside the chapel or the cemetery. What's that all about, are you a writer or a journalist, or something?'

'Nah, I'm not a journalist or a writer, but that's a compliment if you think that. I'm a celebrant, and if you don't know what a Celebrant is ...'

Before Colin could finish his sentence; the man spoke.

'I know what a celebrant is, I've worked here for years. You're one of those people who celebrate the life of the dead person, whatever that means. And some of the poor sods don't have a life that's worth celebrating. I've seen a lot of Celebrants over the years, different kinds, different shapes, different styles, I know them all, but I don't know you. And I don't think you're one of them.'

Colin was a bit embarrassed; this man knew that he was talking nonsense.

'Well, I'm not a celebrant yet, I'm just here to observe and learn. But I know this can be the job for me.'

The fat man started to walk away.

'Well, good luck mate, there are so many Celebrants nowadays. I think you'll really have a hard job getting work from the funeral directors. They have their favourites, and I think a few of them are getting a backhander.'

'Wait a minute, you said you've worked here for years and you know all the people in the funeral business, maybe you can help me out.'

The fat man smiled.

'What makes you think I'd help you? And what's it for me?'

'Well, we could work something out, I'm willing to pay for anything you can help me with. Although I'm a bit skint at the moment, so I might need to pay you in cups of coffee and the occasional doughnut. But we could build it up over time. How about you let me attend some funerals, and keep me out of the way of the grumpy staff. You could give me list of the funeral directors, and arrangers that you know. How about that?'

Colin is anticipating a response while the man is lost in thought.

'Isn't that a simple ask—for a cup of coffee and a doughnut?' Colin tried once more.

'Well, I know working in a cemetery digging holes for dead people, or throwing them inside the oven is a very important job. But is it not a bit boring, and I wouldn't think it pays too much, right? And just think; you'd be helping this poor sad person to make a living. And once business builds up, there would be a few quid in it for you.'

'Okay, okay; you're breaking my heart, it's a deal. You'd bring a tear to a glass eye; are you sure you're in the right profession?'

Colin offered his hand.

'I'm Colin Bott, Civil Celebrant'
'I'm Kevin Stone, grave digger, and crematorium technician extraordinaire.' But Kevin didn't take his hand.

Every day Colin visited the crematorium to attend a funeral service. He sneaked in the back of the crematorium with the help of Kevin to avoid any funeral staff with difficult questions. Sometimes he went to the cemetery, and watched a burial service take place.

Kevin gave him a lot of details about a funeral service, all the procedures and processes. However what Colin was really interested in was how to make contact with the various people in the funeral business, especially the Funeral Directors.

One afternoon, just before the crematorium closed for the day, Colin and Kevin sitting inside drinking coffee.

'I've been here for a couple of weeks now Kevin, and I'm starting to think I am more capable of becoming a grave digger than becoming a celebrant. Mind you, I believe Rod Stewart's first job was as a grave digger. Would that job lead me to become a rock star?'

'I think you've missed the boat on that career, sunshine,' laughed Kevin.

'I've learned enough about funeral service and stuff; you need to give me some contacts. I've been feeding you donuts and pies and coffees every day, I'm running out of money; c'mon when do we see me talking up front looking at a bunch of teary-eyed mourners?'

'Well, it's up to you pal; are you sure you're ready to speak in front of 50, or sometimes 200 people?' said Kevin.

'Listen Kev, if you run out of money, are about to have your electricity cut off, and have the bailiffs at your door, then you would be happy to get up in front of a thousand crying people, and talk about a dead guy or gal.'

Kevin started to feel a bit sorry for Colin.

'Okay. Let's focus on the different kinds of celebrants.

'Why would I need to do that Kevin? All I want to know is how to get people to choose me instead of another Celebrant. I've been round to several Funeral Service offices, and I've spoken to Funeral Directors and Arrangers. And they say things like, "We'll keep you in mind," or "We already work with a few celebrants that we know," or other crap like that. I'm starting to think this job is not for me, and I'm also losing my mind. I keep seeing and talking to dead people, I can't explain that to you mate, I think I'm off my head. But I'm really desperate to get this job. My gran told me that I have a special talent for speaking to people. I even got some kind of award in school, for standing up and speaking to people. I know I can do this job, but what good is it if you have a talent and nobody wants to give you a chance.'

'Listen mate, I'm sorry to hear how desperate you are. But never fear, Kevin is here. If you think you are ready then let's move on. All I'm saying is that before you go to a battle, you need to know your opponent first, and you should know them one by one. Your gran was right, you do have the talent and the ability to speak to people. Use these talents, and I will help you to become the very best Celebrant.

Colin started to get worked up and excited.

'Yes, you bastards, I'm gonna be the best of the best Celebrants in the country! Funeral Directors will beg for my service. All the families will love me and my services, and the dead people will come back to thank me!'

He is interrupted by one of the cleaners in the crematorium.

'Excuse me sir, I'm going to lock up now if you don't mind.'

Colin looked around for Kevin, but he had gone.

The next morning Colin was back at the crematorium and he saw Kevin in the cemetery.

'Where did you disappear to yesterday you bugger? Looks like a busy day today, Kevin? There is a hell of a lot of people in the car park. Who's going in the oven today; must be someone well known, or a hell of a big family.'

'He's not going in the oven, as you say, he will be buried out here, after the service in the Chapel. I just want to make sure that everything is well prepared and ready when they come out here. I want to make it perfect, and that's my duty as a gravedigger.'

'Well, I can see that Kevin, and that's one big deep hole you've dug. Are you just making sure he won't crawl out of his coffin, and ask for his money back. Even Houdini couldn't get out of there especially when it's filled in with tons of soil.

Kevin gives Colin a disdainful look.

'Sorry Kev, I'm just joking.'

'So, why are you looking so serious today, Kevin? yesterday you were all fired up. Has anything happened?

'Nah, I'm ok.'

Kevin stopped digging and put down his shovel. 'Is that a Starbucks coffee you've brought for me? Let's sit down over here and you can tell me your troubles.'

They sat down on a bench, and looked across the cemetery at all the people gathering for the service outside the crematorium.

'Any idea who you're burying today, Kevin?'

'Yes, I do, and guess what, it's an old Celebrant.'

'You're kidding, really? He must have lots of friends and family. I don't think my funeral will be that big, I only know three or four people.' Colin looked a bit sad.

'Well, at least you, or whoever, won't have to spend a lot of money on your funeral, and all that shite. Do you know how much a funeral cost nowadays; it's horrendous, about £4000 to £10000. The flowers alone cost a fortune. If you want a name spelled out, it will cost about £50 a letter. Not so bad if your name was Al or Dad, but if your name is Walloper that's eight letters costing you four hundred quid. Even the dead person will be cursing you for spending all that money, from wherever they are.' Kevin and Colin were laughing.

'I just sometimes get a bit pissed off with all these funeral things Colin. I feel sad for the families, having lost a family member, and of course, having to spend all that money. And I've told you how boring this job can be, so I'm thankful for you for you coming here and take time to talk to me.'

'Well, that's good Kevin, but I'm not just here to entertain you. I'm here to learn and make some contacts so that I can pay my bills. And if you don't help me do that, I'll be pushing you into that hole that you're digging there.'

'Ok pal, hold your horses we're gonna get there. You asked me about the next service and who the deceased was. He is, or should I say was, one of the best celebrants in town. He is also the oldest and the first Celebrant that I know of, funny and respectful. I liked him very much, in fact, we became friends for so many years. He was a great speaker and most families have enjoyed his eulogies. He speaks about the deceased as if he knew them for years. He was my friend Colin, a good friend.'

Colin noticed that Kevin was a bit emotional and teary eyed.

'Ok, let's forget about him; what can you tell me about the other celebrants that are still alive and keep bugging you. You've told me that you don't like most of them, why is that?'

'There are different types, and different ways they annoy me. I'm surprised that so many of them get away with the way they behave. Let me give you some examples. There is one who is a real drama queen. He's a strange little guy with a strong Irish accent. Sometimes you can't make out what he's saying. He's been around for years, and he does a lot of funerals, but I don't think he gets much repeat business.

He's always wearing the same suit, with his fat belly hanging over his trousers, and his shoes could do with a polish. I just don't know what the funeral directors and arrangers see him. Perhaps it's just because he's been around for years and they just use him as a habit. As I said, he's a real drama queen. As often as not, when he's doing a service, he'll start crying, or at least get all teary eyed. He's a big fake. I also know that he's not above slipping a few quid now and again to funeral directors and arrangers. He's never offered me anything in the past, except maybe a fiver at Christmas; miserable little bastard.

'Okay,' said Colin, 'I'll not make those mistakes. I don't want to get into your bad books Kevin. So, who else should I learn from?'

'There's a woman that annoys me; I call her the Hobbit Queen. Every time she does a service, I have to find a box for her to stand on; if not, you'd only see the top of her head when she's standing at the lectern. A seven-year-old girl is probably taller than her. But don't underestimate her, her voice doesn't sound like a Hobbit; it's more like Dumbledore in Harry Potter. To be honest, I like her a bit; she can be a bit of a nippy sweetie, but she has a sense of humour. She drives a big Land Rover with pull out steps which were customized for her so she could easily get in and out of the car.'

'I think I've seen her Kevin. I thought it was a child getting up to do a service. So, who else should I learn from?'

'Well, there's one I call Mr Nicey, Nicey Guy. He's a favourite of the female funeral directors and arrangers. He is very charming and witty; he's always smiling and talking to everyone. He makes me think of an American who is running for President. But not a bit like that wanker, Trump. And of course, like so many politicians, he talks crap all the time. He's immaculately dressed with black patent leather shoes on. He looks like a professional ballroom dancer. And you can smell his cologne a mile away. A lot of the females in the business fancy him for some reason, and they give him work, even although he is more feminine than them. And if the gossip is true, he gets a lot of work from one funeral director in the town. And I'm not talking about a woman; you know what I mean Colin?'

'Yeah; I think I met him one time, and he was

very interested in me, but not for my skills as a speaker. Do you know what *I* mean Kevin?'

'Yes, I do Colin, and I suggest you keep away from him. There's another celebrant they call "Dead Man Walking." Are you familiar with the film of that name, or any films with zombies. Well, this is one of them. He is a very tall thin pale man with lank black hair, and the deceased people he's dealing with look a lot healthier than him. He speaks very slowly and quietly, and you will see people fall asleep while listening to his eulogy. If you met him in a dark alley one night, you'd shit your pants. He's not a threat to you, but he gets work from some funeral directors. Probably the old-fashioned ones that want someone leading the service who look like death themselves.'

'Yeah, I don't understand it sometimes, why would a funeral director choose him. It looks like he would make the families even more upset than they already are. So, who else am I up against?'

'Well, priests, church ministers and vicars, have to be considered as your competitors. There is not much you can do about that, as they are usually chosen by the family. If the deceased was a member of a church. Or maybe some families, although they don't go to church, or are religious, are scared that there is a god and their dearly departed won't get into heaven. I don't think they get paid to conduct a service, but you're expected to make a donation to their church. They don't talk much about the life of the deceased, but more about all the god stuff; sermons and prayers and hymns and other mumbo jumbo. The funeral directors hate them, because the service takes so long, and they have to hang about outside. And watch yourself, although the religious people appear to be nice to you, they hate celebrants.'

'I understand what you mean, Kevin. I've been to religious funerals, and I've come out of the church or the crematorium, more depressed than I was when I went in.'

'You'll hear a lot of people refer to you as a Humanist, Colin. They're not a lot different from a Celebrant, they are almost on the same page. Their services are completely non-religious. Humanists are concerned about the here and now and believe this is the only life we have. They don't sing hymns at the funeral, and no prayers. But as a Civil Celebrant, Colin, you can. Although the family members arranging a funeral may not be religious, their mother or father or grandparents may have been, and they may want a hymn and a prayer. So that is an advantage for you Colin.'

'Yeah, my mum and dad went to church, and they sent me to Sunday school. So, although I'm not a church goer, I'm perfectly willing to have a hymn or a prayer.'

'Right Colin, the last person to conduct a service could be a Satanist.'

'A what?' said a shocked Colin.

'You must be joking'

'Hahaha, relax Colin, I'm only kidding. But with all the nonsense going on nowadays, I wouldn't be surprised to see a Satanist Celebrant sometime in the future.'

'You're full of shite Kevin, I don't know whether to believe you or not. But thanks for opening my eyes to what's going on in the funeral world. I don't think that it's complicated, and I'm sure I can do this job. Besides, I tried other jobs and nothing worked for me. I believe I have the gift to communicate with people, living or non-living - I think.'

'I bet you do, Colin.'

CHAPTER FIVE

Mrs. Chan

It was early morning and Colin opened his front door to find Lucifer. As usual, he was nowhere to be found.

'Bloody cat; he's gonna get run down one day and then he'll never come back. Right, let's check the emails and the phone messages.'

Colin stared at his old laptop, scrolling down all the junk email.

'Nothing as usual; I'm getting fed up with this. And I'm fed up going to that crematorium to see Kevin. He only wants to see me now for a free coffee and doughnuts. The old bugger will be wondering where I am now. I'd go round to his house if I knew where he lived, because that crematorium and graveyard is getting very depressing. And here I am talking to myself again like a fucking lunatic.'

That evening, Colin put some crushed up bread in Lucifer's bowl, and poured some of the oil from a can of sardines over it.

'Okay, that's our dinner, tinned sardines for me, and the residue for Lucifer. I'm getting really fed up with these ready meals. The chicken dishes have the constancy of a school rubber eraser, and anything that has meat in it was probably the remains of a racehorse that died of old age. I don't even want to think about anything that has the word pork in its list of ingredients. Let's see if I can find that bloody cat.'

Colin couldn't find Lucifer anywhere; he searched the whole house and called out the door again.

'Hey! Luci, puss, puss, where are you, here's your din, dins. I've made a sumptuous dish salmon with a touch of virgin coconut oil, with catnip on the side. Come and get it. Where is that devil cat again? Maybe he's up on the roof again, looking for a bit of pussy. Not that any other cat would be interested in him. He's a grumpy bugger, and I know if I try to reprimand him, he'll scratch my eyes out. He bloody scares me.'

Colin went into the bedroom still searching for the cat. Suddenly there was a bit of a commotion outside the flat and then a loud thump.

'What the hell was that? That'll be Mrs Chan watching TV again. I know she turns up the volume on that big TV of hers, just to annoy me. Maybe that's her fighting with the Avengers, doing a bit of Kung Fu.'

Suddenly, Lucifer appeared through the open window, leapt into the bedroom, and landed on

Colin's back digging his claws in.

'What the fuck! Luci! I told you not to do that! Bloody cat!'

Colin closed the window, and looked around to see if he could find out where the loud thump came from: was it inside or outside.

'Go get your food in the kitchen, you silly cat. And don't ask me for cat food because we don't have any, and you and I are going to die soon if I don't get a job.'

Colin took two of his sleeping pills, and climbed into bed. This was the only way that he could sleep, and stop worrying about his financial situation.

The next morning Colin's bleary eyes opened to find a golden cat with a waving arm, sitting on his bedside table.

'How the hell did that get there? I know what that is, it's a Fortune Cat, or Maneki Neko. It's a lucky cat charm and they are very popular in Japanese and Chinese cultures. It's a talisman that is believed to attract good luck and fortune for its owners. Well, don't I know a lot of things, probably because I've been in enough Chinese restaurants in my life. But how the hell did it get in here?'

Colin pulled on a bathrobe and dragged himself into the kitchen, looking for something for breakfast.

'No bread, no coffee no cereal; what a fucking life.'

He headed for the convenience store across the road and picked up some bread, milk and a small jar of the cheapest coffee. He stood in the small queue waiting to pay Ali, the Pakistani owner of the shop. He was standing at the till and doing his usual - chatting up the female customers. Ali is a bit like Colin, single and desperate.

Ali tells his female customers that he lives alone in a beautiful house, has a nice car and a business that brings in good money. He thinks he looks like a younger version of the handsome Imran Khan, the Pakistani cricketer and politician. However, he has a face that looks like a squashed rusty tin can. And his breath stinks as if he'd eaten the dogfood that was in the can, and was well passed its sell by date.

One of the women in the queue turned around, looked at Colin in his bathrobe and gave him a smile.

'My apologies for my shabby attire,' said Colin, a bit sarcastically.

It's my manservant's day off and I needed some milk for my cat. I'm a pussy lover, and I don't want him to miss his breakfast. He is my priority you know, and this bread is also for the him, sweet cat.'

Colin noticed that this woman was just the type that Ali would like to get his claws into; so, he decided to save her.

'When you get to the front of the queue, I suggest you wear a mask covering your mouth and nose. Only have your eyes showing. Ali, the owner had covid last week and it's very contagious. He shouldn't be here; in fact, he should be in hospital and away from us.'

When the woman was about to pay, Ali was leering at her with his tin can smile. He gave her the change, and was about to use his chat up line. When the woman immediately pulled her mask over her mouth and nose. And with not even looking at Ali she hurriedly walked away.

'See that Colin, I paid so much money for my dentist to fix my teeth, and I listened to your advice about my stinky breath. But I told you it's a natural smell in my country. That's because we eat so many onions and garlic. Did you see that woman walking away before I had a chance to speak to her; women still not wanting me mate, absolutely rude!'

Ali was shaking his head while checking the price of Colin's stuff. He just smiled to himself, and waited for Ali to finish.

'Did you hear the news this morning Colin' said Ali? Or did you hear anything last night? You must have; there was a robbery last night in your building.'

Colin was confused.

'What robbery are you talking about, I was sleeping like a baby last night. I took some sleeping pills before I went to bed and I slept right through. Never heard a thing. The only thing I heard earlier on, was Mrs Chan's loud TV.'

'Well. I don't think her TV will bother you anymore. She was robbed last night and her body was found on the stairs.'

'Oh my god! Was she shot or something; I'm sure I would have heard that.'

'Listen mate; the police were everywhere in your building last night. When they found her on the stairway, they reckoned that she had tried to run after the robbers and fell down the stairs, or maybe she was pushed. Whatever it is, the police will find it difficult to arrest someone for murder. I don't know the exact story mate, it's in the paper. Here's the newspaper read it.'

Colin looked at the front page of the local newspaper. The headline was "Chinese Woman Found Dead in Robbery Gone Wrong". There was a picture of Mrs Chan on the front page, sitting on the sofa in her flat, smiling at the camera.

'Holy fuck! She's got that bloody golden cat sitting on the table beside her.'

'Chinese people find these golden cats very lucky,' said Ali. 'Didn't work very well for her though eh! Is there anything else you need today, Colin; how about a lottery ticket. Maybe your luck will be better today. Better than Mrs Chan's anyway. There you go, £6.75; would you like a bag, Colin?'

'Put it on my tab.'

Colin grabbed the milk and bread and ran out the door.

Ali called after him.

'Hey Colin; it's time you paid your tab, you miserable bastard. I'm not running a charity shop you know.'

Colin ran up the stairs to his flat, avoiding the chalk marks on the stairs where Mrs Chan's body had been found. He didn't notice it before when he went to the shop, he was too busy looking at his phone.

'Lucifer, where are you? What have you done?'

Lucifer was sitting on the small dining table, looking at Colin in attack mode. He didn't want to be reprimanded if he had done something wrong.

'You thief! You're in trouble cat; how did you manage to get Mrs. Chan's golden cat, where is it? Where did you hide it?'

Colin was getting really worked up, and he was panicking. He was running around the flat trying to find the golden cat that was on his bedside table that morning.

Suddenly there was heavy knocking on the front door.

'Hello - Police! Anyone home.'

'Fuck it!'

Colin ran around the flat, still looking for the golden cat and trying to tidy the place up.

'Coming; won't be a minute!'

He was muttering to himself.

'Calm down for fuck's sake; you've done nothing wrong.'

He opened the door to two obvious detective police officers.

'Good morning, sir, sorry to bother you,' said one of them.

'Can I confirm who you are?'

'C...Co...Colin Bott, the owner, sorry tenant of this flat.'

'Which is it sir? We don't want to get things confused.'

'It's tenant, and I'm a bit nervous about police coming to the door. It's never good news, is it?'

'That's understandable sir; my colleague and I would like to ask you a few questions about last night's incident, if that's okay?'

'Yes, yes of course. What incident exactly, are you talking about?'

'There was an incident last night; can we

come in, sorry to bother you but it won't take long.'

'Oh, ok, where's my manners; of course, come in. Sorry about the mess, I have a cat, he is a messy cat likes to play around, and I haven't been well these past weeks, no time to clean.'

Two police officers, a middle age man and a woman walked into the room and looked around.

'I am Detective Sergeant McGonagle and this is Detective Constable Patel.'

Colin noticed that the Policewoman's eyes were scanning his flat like she was looking for something, and he started to get nervous. All he can think about is, 'where's that bloody golden cat?'

The police officer was talking to Colin about the incident and Colin was pretending to listen, but his eyes keep looking at detective Patel as she walked towards his bedroom.

'Do you mind if I have a look in the bedroom?
'Eh, nope, not at all, please, please just help yourself go on you can check the place, there's nothing to hide here.'

'Excuse me, why did you say there's nothing to hide here, do you think we are looking for something?' said Detective Sergeant McGonagle.

'No, no, what I meant was that I read this morning in the newspaper that there are things missing from Mrs. Chan's flat. I suppose it's better to look at every flat in the building. You, you never know; sometimes the killer is just around the corner.'

'And what makes you say that Mr. Bott?' McGonagle looked straight into Colin's face.

'Nothing, I mean that is always the scene in the movie, right?'

McGonagle continued to look straight into Colin's eyes, and he tried to avoid the stare; he walked towards the kitchen and the detective followed him.

'Would you like to have a coffee or tea?' Colin started to calm down. He opened the top cupboard to get a teacup without waiting for a reply.

'What is your relationship with Mrs. Chan, I mean as a neighbour; what can you tell me about her?'

'Oh, Mrs. Chan, she is a wonderful woman, we get along really well. In fact, we are very close, but not that close as in having a relationship if you know what I mean. It's mutual, it's like mother and son.'

'Ok go on, what else?'

'Well, she always said hello to me every time we bumped into each other in the stairway, and we pass the time of day.'

Colin remembered that whenever they bumped to each other, in the park, going for groceries, or in Marco's shop, Mrs. Chan always said the same thing to him in Chinese. And he always replied to her, 'same to you too Mrs. Chan.'

Whatever the words meant, Colin didn't care. It could have been anything. something nasty or rude. Although, thinking about all the times he met Mrs Chan, part of him felt a bit sad. But another part of him felt glad that she wouldn't' annoy him anymore. He had a little smile to himself.

'Mr Bott, hello! Sorry to disturb your thoughts. When was the last time you spoke or saw Mrs. Chan?'

'Last week I think it was, when we bumped into each other on the stairs. As you've probably noticed, the stairs are very narrow and a bit worn. Anybody could slip there at any time if they weren't careful. I'm not saying that Mrs. Chan couldn't see properly, because of her slitty eyes, she probably had poor eyesight because of her age; I think she was over 70.

'I thought you two were close why don't you don't know her age Mr. Bott?'

'Oh, eh, I mean, I never asked. It's rude to ask people their age, isn't it. We never mentioned it. Maybe she was shy or she wanted to be private. Yup, that's it. She was a very private person and a very quiet neighbour also.'

Colin started to realise that he's babbling like an idiot.

'I found something,' said detective Patel

who came out from Colin's bedroom.

'Shit!'

Colin dropped his cup. 'Sorry about that.'

Colin's hand started to shake.

Patel whispered in the McGonagle's ear.

'Mr. Bott, where were you last night?' asked Patel.

Colin closed his eyes and tried to stay calm.

'I was here sleeping the entire night.'

'I found something in your bedroom Mr. Bott' the Patel stared into Colin's face.

Colin started to sweat. He was thinking,

'I'm going to jail; my life is over.'

Patel put the bottle of pills on the table.

'Do you have a prescription for this medicine Mr. Bott? According to the date on the bottle, it's already expired and it's dangerous to take these tablets. It's not safe to take sleeping pills when they're out of date; you might be sleeping for the rest of your life. No wonder you didn't bother to open the door last night when we try to contact you.'

Colin couldn't speak, no words seem to generate from his mouth; is brain is scattered in every part of his head. The detective McGonagle stood up.

'Anyway, we better go now, thanks for your cooperation; be sure to lock your door properly and let us know if you find out anything that would help us regarding Mrs. Chan's incident.'

'No worries, I'll make sure to let you know if I find the killer.'

McGonagle stopped at the door and turned round, looking a bit surprised.

'What makes you say that Mr. Bott. Is there something you're not telling us? And you seem very nervous.'

'Eh, nope, nope. It's just that all of this is very upsetting, and I'm just a concerned neighbour.'

'Well, don't worry Mr Bott, we'll be doing our best to bring the perpetrator to justice'

The two detectives stepped out the door, and before he closed it, Colin heard McGonagle speaking on the radio.

'Officer Brown, can you check Mrs. Chan's place again, and see if you think anything is missing, please double check, copy and check flat 64?'

'10-4' replied Officer Brown.

Colin was starting to panic, where the hell was the golden cat?

He was about to close the door.

'Excuse me Mr. Bott your flat is number 65, is that right?'

'Yes, that's right, number 64 is just along the corridor and round the corner. I need to go officer thank you.'

The two policemen seemed to be satisfied as they walked away. Colin immediately locked his door; he was still shaking.

Colin grabbed his phone and called Marco.

'Pick up Marco.'

The voicemail message clicked - 'Hello, thank you for calling, Marco is very busy right now. Please leave a message when you hear the beep.'

'Shit! Marco it's Colin; the Police are on their way to your flat. If you're there no matter what happens, keep them busy, talk to them. Hold them for as long as you can, I just need to do something thanks.'

He put down the phone.

'Where the hell is the fucking cat! Luci! Where the hell are you!'

Lucifer was lying on his bed on his back, and Colin noticed the shiny golden cat beside him on the bed. It looked like he was trying to hide it.

'There it is, you fool!'

Colin picked up the figurine cat and looked out at Mrs. Chan's window, just opposite his window, 'With a few steps and one jump I could easily get inside kitchen, thought the brave Colin.

'Lucifer, why don't you put it back where you

got it, c'mon you can do it, just put it back in Mrs. Chan house, I won't tell anyone, c'mon.' Lucifer curled up in his bed and fell asleep.

Colin checked out Mrs Chan's kitchen window; he could see a small gap where he could get a grip and open the window.

'Right Colin, you can do this; just crawl round that edge, open the window and go in with this bloody cat. If Tom Cruise can do it, so can Colin Bott. If I don't return this cat, and the police find out I have it, they'll blame me for stealing it, and probably bumping her off.'

He opened the bedroom window, and started to crawl along the edge. He then realised this was not such a good idea, especially as it has started to rain and the wind had picked up. Colin was muttering to himself.

'Don't look down, don't look down. It's only two floors, if you fall you won't kill yourself, but probably break most of the bones in your body. But at least I won't be in jail for stealing this cat or murdering Mrs Chan'

Colin had to crawl past one of Marco's windows, and he could see him inside, walking around with a towel around his waist. He was obviously just out of the shower and entertaining himself singing an Italian Aria. Colin tried to attract his attention without making too much noise or falling off the ledge.

'Hey Pavarotti, I'm out here, turn around, and stop that wailing.'

Colin knocked on the window and Marco nearly jumped out of his skin.

'What the fuck! What are you doing Colin, you peeping Tom. Are you trying to catch me in the nudie?'

Marco opened the window.

'Don't be so bloody stupid Marco, seeing you in nude would put me off your fish n chips for life. I'm trying to get into Mrs Chan's flat. I'll explain to you later. Check your phone, I left you a message; the Police are probably at your door now. You probably won't hear the doorbell with that racket you're making. Keep them busy and hold on to them for as long as you can. Give me a chance to return this golden cat and get back into my own flat.'

Marco heard someone knocking on his door; he listened to Colin's voice mail, and gave him the thumbs up.

Colin tapped on the window and signalled to Marco to close the blinds so that the Police couldn't see him outside. Luckily Marco heard him tapping and closed the blinds. Colin crawled round the ledge to Mrs Chan's window. The window was an old-style sash sliding window, and it was stuck. Colin was also scared he would slip and fall to the ground below.

Eventually, with sweat pouring off him, he was in. He walked around the empty cold flat trying to find the exact spot where he seen the golden cat positioned in the newspaper picture. He found it, put the cat down and ran to the kitchen window. He was starting to get scared that anyone would see him in the flat.

'Fuck!!!'

The window had slipped down and it was stuck again. In a blind panic, Colin pulled and pulled the window.

'Better make sure I don't break it, that would definitely drop me in the shit.'

He nearly fell through the window when his phone rang, with the dulcet tones of Michael Bublé and Sway.

'Hello, hello,' Colin whispered. It was Marco.
'Colin, they've gone, and they're heading back to your place.'
He could see Colin from his window, running around in Mrs Chan's flat like a headless chicken.

'Hide Colin, run Colin, you are going to jail if they catch you in there.'
'For fuck's sake Marco I can't hide here, there's nowhere to hide. I need to get back to my own flat.'

Colin's fear gave him that extra shot of

adrenaline and the strength to pull up the window, climb out, and scurry round the ledge like a scared rat. Once in his own flat, he could hear the two detectives talking in the hallway. He was tempted to ignore them, but thought the better of it. Wiping the sweat from his brow, he opened the door.

'Hello again officers, did you find Marco, was he of any help to you.'
'Hello again Mr Bott, have you been working out; you're looking a bit warm.'
'Yeah, just doing a few exercises to keep fit.'
'Have you been outside? That looks like bird shit on your shoulder.'
'What, no, eh, I just leant out the window to throw some bread to the birds. Just shows you what they think of me eh.'

McGonagle spoke, 'We talked to your neighbour, nice man, he was very helpful. He called down to his shop and someone brought up fish and chips for our lunch. It's not every day you get that on the job. I've had a few fish suppers thrown at me in my day, but not ones I could eat.'
Colin smiled.

'Well, he is a very friendly neighbour, all of us are friendly here very close to each other so you don't need to worry about us. Oh, by the way, are you going to Mrs. Chan's flat today?'
'Yes, we just need to lock up her flat. My

colleague says that they forgot to lock it up this morning and we need to have a final check around her house.'

'So, it's been unlocked all day. Somebody could've gone in there and taken something.'

'No worries, sir; I'm sure no one around here would want to go in there. We'll be off, and if you think of anything, please get in touch.'

Colin closed the door and started banging his head off the wall.

'What an idiot I am; nearly killing myself falling off the ledge when I could've walked round and into the flat.'

Colin's phone rang.

'Hello Colin, it's Chris Thatcher at Thatcher's Funeral Directors. Are you available to do a service for us next week?'

'Yes, yes. I mean hold on while I check my diary.'

Colin looked at the blank wall, knowing the diary was also blank.

'Yes, that will be okay. Can you send me the details and I'll contact the client.'

Colin danced round the room in delight, his first job. This was not a bad day after all for Colin.

CHAPTER SIX

Hello Irene Reid

Colin rang the doorbell on an old Victorian style house in a posh part of town. A man in his late thirties opened the door.

'Hello Mr Daforth, my name is Colin Bott, and I'm a Civil Celebrant.

'Hello Mr Bott, pleased to meet you. Come in, come in, we were expecting you.'

Mr Daforth's voice was posh and educated, but warm and friendly.

Colin guessed he must be solicitor or a doctor, and he felt a bit uncomfortable. Colin spoke to himself.

'C'mon Colin, get a grip of yourself; he's no better than you and you need to look and sound professional.'

He entered a expansive hallway and followed Mr Daforth into a large living room.

'Good to meet you, Colin; we weren't expecting you for another twenty minutes.'

The man looked at his watch.
'But that's okay, have a seat.'

Colin quickly realised that time was

important to this man, and regretted coming so early.

'Sorry if I'm a bit early, I can come back later if you are busy.'

'No, please it's ok, it's just that my wife is taking a shower, but she will be with you in a few minutes. So, you are a Celebrant Colin; let me introduce myself. I am Henry Daforth.'

He held out his hand to Colin.

'That's a nice name. does that mean there was a Henry the first, second and third in your family?'

The stupid joke was not appreciated and Colin regretted it immediately.

'No; I said Henry Da Forth as in Forth Bridge.'

Henry gave Colin a sardonic smile.

'Oh, I do apologise.'

Colin cursed himself – 'shut up you stupid bastard, you'll ruin everything.'

'It's ok I get that a lot. Sometimes I just let it pass and let people think I'm an aristocrat. But I'm just a surgeon.'

'Just a surgeon; that's great. I'm just a celebrant.' Colin was tempted to say – 'can I have the names of any of any of your mistakes that don't make it,' but he bit his tongue.

'I will go and check on my wife and let her know you are here. She shouldn't be long.'

'No worries, I will just wait here.'

Colin was sitting comfortably in an arm chair admiring the pictures and ornaments around the room. He turned around and was startled when he came face to face with little Chinese child of about four years old. She pointed and spoke to him.

Colin looked around.

'I'm sorry, are you talking to me? I don't understand you. I don't speak Chinese or whatever language that was, but maybe you are saying bad words to me.'

Colin heard a voice behind him.

'I'm sorry for my daughter, yes she's Chinese and so I am. Hi, I'm Lina and that is my 4-year-old daughter Irene.'

'So, you must be Mrs. Daforth, Henry's wife. Nice to meet you.'

'And you must be Mr Bott, the Celebrant.'

'Yes, I'm Colin Bott, but please call me Colin. You have a lovely daughter, and she was just telling me something which I couldn't understand.'

'Oh, she wants her monkey stuffed toy. I think you are sitting on it.'

Colin look around.

'Oops, I'm sorry about that, here's your little monkey, Irene. I thought you were calling me a monkey.'

Colin handed over the stuffed toy monkey to Irene.

Lina whispered in Chinese to her daughter.

'I told you to stop saying to people that they are monkeys. Now go to your room.'

'Bye Mr. Colin,' said the smiling little Irene

'She can speak English; she is just winding you up. I think she likes you,' said Lina.

'No worries, Mrs Daforth, and my condolences for your mother.

'Thank you, Colin. It's all very sad, even more so bearing in mind how she died. But I don't want to talk about that now, it's much too distressing.'

'Well, it's good to meet you, and I would just like to find out a bit more about your mother, Mrs Reid, which will enable me to write a draft eulogy. And once I've done that, I'll send it to you for chucking, sorry, I mean checking.'

Colin is a bit nervous because this is his first ever visit to the family of the deceased.

'Would you like a cup of tea or coffee Colin?' Asked Mrs Daforth.

'Yes, thank you; that would be nice.'

'Well just relax for a few minutes and I'll be right back. And please call me Lina'

Colin was fidgeting, he was still nervous and kept glancing at his notes checking the questions to ask. He stood up and had a walk around the large sitting room.

'They're posh, so they probably call it a Drawing Room,' he muttered to himself.

Mrs Daforth was taking her time making the tea, so Colin had a good look round the sitting room. It was furnished with expensive looking antique furniture, some of it obviously oriental.

'These people are loaded,' thought Colin.
'They've probably inherited all this stuff and the house from their family. Look at all these photographs in silver frames. Maybe I could increase my fee, 'he thought.
'Behave yourself Colin, this is your first job, don't fuck it up.'

Colin scanned the pictures in the frames. He let out a muffled scream.

'Aaaaaahhhh!'

He spun round to find Mrs Daforth standing in front of him with a tray of tea and coffee. She screamed at the same time.

'Aaaaaaahhhh! What's wrong Colin?'

She nearly dropped the tray.

'Nothing, nothing; I...I just thought I saw someone I knew.'

Colin felt a wave of nausea and a cold sweat

start to run down the back of his neck. He couldn't believe what he had just seen in a picture frame on the fireplace.

'Sorry! my fault, sorry to scare you, Lina.' Colin was helping her with the tray when her husband suddenly appeared from the hallway.

'Is everything ok, what had happened to you guys?' he asked.

'It's my fault, I didn't mean to frighten your wife. I was just looking at a picture in a frame on the fireplace.'

'Do you mean the picture of my Mother Colin? She wasn't that scary.'

Lina was laughing. She took the picture from above the fireplace.

'I thought maybe my mother's ghost was visiting us already. This is my mother, Colin; I'd like you to meet Mrs. Irene Chan Reid.' And you are going to conduct her funeral service next week.'

'Are you ok Colin, you look pale?'

Mr Daforth took the tray from Lina and laid it down on a the side table.

'I'm ok just a bit confused. I thought that your mother was Mrs. Reid. I wasn't expecting that Lina's mother is Mrs. Chan, not Mrs Reid, so I'm a bit lost here.'

Colin realised that he was starting to talk gibberish and behaving like a fool.

'Sorry about the confusion Colin, that's

why I let you speak to my wife alone because I know nothing about my mother-in-law, we were never close to each other. Especially when Lina had a big argument with her mother before we were married. She was not happy that her daughter would marry an Englishman just like she did.'

'Let me explain Colin,' said Lina.

'This is a family matter but I don't think there's anything wrong in sharing it with you. My mother was married to an Englishman which was her second marriage. That is why her name is Irene Chan Reid. I named my daughter Irene after her. Anyway, they brought me here to the UK when I was 10 years old. My stepdad and my mother had a bad relationship. He was jealous about everything, and they were always fighting. Eventually she left him and raised me as a single parent. That was the start of her hatred for every Englishman in this country. And of course, she was not happy when I started a relationship with an Englishman and eventually married him.

After that, there was a breakdown in our relationship; she did not want to communicate. She did not want to see me or even her granddaughter Irene. I know where she lives and I tried to communicate with her, but she is a pig-headed woman. Every gift that I sent her, on her birthday, she returned. I was mad at her; so, on her 70th birthday last year, I sent the most valuable gift to her. It was the necklace that she gave to me on my 7th birthday. This was the necklace that my father gave to her when they were married. It is a gold moon and stars necklace with my parent's initial I and B, for Irene and Ben.'

Colin was still a bit shocked but was starting to calm down and taking it all in.

'Excuse me, Colin, are you not going to take notes of what I've been saying?' said Lina.

'Oh, yeah, of course, of course, I was just paying so much attention to your story, I'm interested, please go on, I will take notes now.'

Colin started writing in his notepad.

'Ok, so after I sent her the necklace, she did not send it back to me. I wanted her to get mad or say something. I knew that she would not be happy, and she would feel disrespectful returning something so important and emotionally valuable. I just wanted her to communicate with me again. But she didn't, she just kept my necklace, never said a word, a letter or an email. That is the last time that I communicated with her.'

Lina started crying and her husband Henry put his arms around her. Colin wanted to change the atmosphere the room so that Lina would not be upset.

Colin started to ask questions about Mrs. Chan's life. When she was a child, where she grew up, her family back in China, her education, and what she liked about being a mother to Lina. It took about an hour to finish their conversation.

'Thank for your time and this information,' said Colin. I will now write a draft eulogy and send it to you for checking in the next few days. I will do my best to incorporate all these notes into a good Eulogy for your Mother Lina.'

'Thank you, Colin,' said Lina.

'Let me show you out.'

As they were walking along the hallway, a Persian cat appeared and started to play around Colin's legs.

'Oh, sorry about that, stop it, Millie. She's my daughter's cat,' said Lina

Colin reached down to stroke the cat.

'Hello there pussy; I mean Millie, you are such a lovely cat. Do you know what, I have a cat at home too. He's not a very friendly cat. His name's Lucifer, which kind of tells it all. That's why Mrs Chan is always running after him with a cleaver. She keeps telling me – "Keep your bloody cat away from my kitchen or I'll kill you both hahaha."

The couple looked at each other and gave Colin a confusing look. He realised he had gone too far.

'Did I say Mrs Chan; I'm sorry. I meant to say Mrs Chen who is a Chinese neighbour of mine. Mrs. Chen, not Chan, it's Chen. Colin realised he was starting to talk gibberish and behaving like a fool again.

'Anyway, I better go now, cheers, see you next week at the funeral, bye, bye.'

Henry and Lina closed the door and stared at each other.

'Are you sure he is the right celebrant to do the Eulogy for your mum, Lina.?'

'I think he is; anyway, Irene and Millie like him, what can go wrong?' said Lina with a shrug.

CHAPTER SEVEN

"How to Get Rid of Demons for Dummies"

Colin found himself driving the car in heavy traffic, heading for home. He was talking to himself in the car.

'Boy, was I glad to get out of that house. They don't know that was my first home visit with a family. They probably think I'm just an idiot.'

As he was walking to his flat, he spotted Marco washing dirt off the chip shop window.

'Hey Marco, why is it such a mess?

'Bloody hooligans were pelting the window with eggs and dirt, and God knows what else. Just because I don't give them any free chips. They know I give the old folk some chips or the occasional pie. But there is nothing for them; they spend their money on cheap alcohol and vape cigarettes, and go around causing trouble. And now I can't find the sponge I was washing the window with. Mia must have taken it. Anyway, Colin, how was your day today my friend?'

'Well, it's time to celebrate Marco, I've got my first Funeral Service. I've just been to see the family, and they were most impressed with me. I am officially a Celebrant.'

'That's great Colin; see what I told you, your

time will come, and you'll get all the dead people out there. They will come to you, at least their relatives will, and you will be busy all the time.' Marco was shaking Colin's hand when Mia arrived.

'Hey Marco, there's telephone call for you. A crazy person who just had delivery from Justa Eat. She saying she no order a battered sponge and chips, you idiot.'

'Oh shit; one of the window washing sponges must have fallen in the deep fat fryer again. I better go.' Marco ran away in a panic.

'See you later Colin. Mia, be sure to give Colin free chips, he got his first funeral work today.'

'So, you must be happy now Colin, you got the job. I'm happy for you; is this a big money job?' Mia was smiling.

'Eh, not really Mia, but it sure helps pay my bills. It's a start, but I'm not sure if I will get another one, we'll see.'

'So, this is not a permanent job, eh?'

Mia looked disappointed.

'No, it's more of a self-employed job really. So, no work, no pay. But we'll see; it's a start and it's better than nothing at the moment. And I'm confident work will come along.

'Well good for you Colin, I like your positivity. It's like my papa used to say - no pain no gain.'

'I'd better get going Mia. I think Lucifer will be glad to see me; I forgot to leave him food today, so I am expecting a scratch. See you later Mia.'

'See ya later crocodile.' Mia waved her hand.

Colin was smiling. 'It's alligator you daft woman,' as he waved back and walked through the door leading to his flat.

Later that night, Colin was tossing and turning in bed, unable to sleep. He got up, walked to the kitchen, and started to make some herbal tea. He picked up his mug of camomile tea and sat by the window looking out at the traffic below.

It was fairly quiet at this time in the morning, and there was no smell of fish and chips coming up from the shop below.

'What the fuck!' He nearly dropped his tea when he thought he saw Mrs Chan in the window of her flat. She looked like she was alive. He hurriedly pulled the curtain across the window and checked it was locked.

'What the hell is wrong with me? Why do I keep seeing dead people?'

Colin heard a crash in the kitchen.
'What the hell was that?'

He slowly walked into the kitchen.

'Lucifer, is that you? Luci, it's past your bedtime, you should be sleeping, Lucifer...'

Colin turned on the light in the kitchen, startling Lucifer who bumped into the container containing his dried cat food and sent it all flying across the kitchen floor.

'You, stupid cat! That's a month's worth of food all over the floor. We are trying to watch the money here, so I will have to sweep that up and put it back in the container, and you will eat it.'

Lucifer made a strange noise and looked like he was in attack mode. He was looking straight at Colin.

'Now, Luci! Do not give me one of your attack moves. That is not nice, calm down, you devil cat, calm down.'

Colin was a bit scared; he was holding a clothes hanger and pointing it at Lucifer while slowly walking backward. He had never seen Lucifer so angry before. But it looked like he was defending himself from something, not attacking. He let out a roar, and jumped towards Colin –

'Raaarrrrrrr !'

Colin, put his hands to his head protecting his face from Lucifer's attack. But Lucifer jumped over him and seemed to run after something or someone behind Colin. Colin looked around wondering where he'd gone.

'Bloody cat, always scares me to death.'

Colin turned off the lights in the kitchen and jumped into his bed and pulled the duvet over his head, just like he did when he was frightened as a child. All he could hear was his heartbeat and his breath. Suddenly he heard the sound of Lucifer's ball toy which had a little bell inside. He was flipping it into the air and chasing it around the room.

'Not again Lucifer, give me a break. Leave the ball alone and let me get to sleep.'

Colin pulled the duvet from his face, and found himself looking straight into the eyes of Lucifer as he sat on the floor. In the darkness all Colin could see was the big green eyes glowing in the dark and staring back at him. Out of the corner of his eye he saw the golden cat glowing in the dark.

'Colin sat straight up in bed.
'What the fuck! How did that thing get back in here? He then heard what he thought was breathing. He sat up in bed, switched on the bedside light, and looked up to see Mrs. Chan's decaying body sticking to the ceiling, smiling at him.

'I told you I would scare the shit of you someday!' She said and laughed in this strange hysterical way.

Colin fainted back on the bed.

The following morning Colin was running fast up the stairs with a bag of groceries. Marco was on the way down and they bumped into each other.

'Out of my Marco, no time to talk thank you very much!'

'What's wrong Colin my friend is everything ok?'

Colin was trying to open his flat door.

'I'm ok Marco; talk to you later, bye.'

Marco shrugged his shoulder and continued down the stairs.
Colin opened the front door and went straight to the kitchen. He was going through all the drawers looking for something.

'Where are the bloody matches? I'm sure I have candles somewhere.'

He found the matches and a candle and headed into his bedroom. He opened the window and looked straight ahead at Mrs Chan's kitchen window. He put various bits and pieces on his window ledge. One candle, a plate, some sage, pots and pans, and a bottle of Holy water. He was holding a book – "How to Get Rid of Demons for Dummies".

He lit the candle and put the plate of sage on the window sill.

'Let's see if you can scare me again, you devil woman. I tried to be nice to you when you were alive, but this time I won't let you scare me again. Oh no Mrs. Chan, come and get me if you dare.'

He started reading the book out loud.

"Follow the instructions carefully or suffer the consequences". 'What the hell is this; what kind of consequences? This is crap; what can go wrong if you don't follow instructions?'

Colin continued reading the book out loud.

"This book is for Dummies like you; if you don't follow the instructions the Demons will come after you".

'For fuck's sake; I'm bloody well following the instructions. Ok let's start again, Number one - burn sage. Yes, yes; it's there on the plate.

Number two - make sure to open the door and the window so the demons can get out. Right, what's next - let the sage burn for 30 seconds before you blow the flame out. Allow the sage to smoulder and the smoke will cleanse the space of negative energy.'

Colin wafted the smoke into the corners of the bedroom, the living room and the kitchen, allowing it to reach all the nooks and crannies. He was moving around holding the plate with the smouldering sage.

However, he didn't notice that some of the sage fell onto the bedroom carpet and started burning. The smoke detector alarm went off and he noticed that there was a lot of smoke coming from his bedroom. He started to panic.

'Damn it to hell!'

He looked around for something to put water into, grabbed a big plant pot and pulled the plant out. He filled the pot with water from the kitchen sink and ran to the bedroom. But the plant pot had a hole in it and there was water running everywhere all over the floor.

'Aw, shit! Shit! Shit.'

There wasn't enough water to put out the fire so Colin pulled the duvet off the bed and smothered the fire on the carpet. He was sitting on the floor, exasperated. He picked up the Dummies book and started to read again.

'Avoid negativity and control your emotions. Demons will continue to come to you if you have much anger in your thoughts. Ha, ha, ha. I will kill whoever wrote this book'

Colin turned the page again.

'So, what's next? Sprinkle holy water around your home; holy water will drive away demons. Visit your local Catholic church and ask them if you can have a bottle of holy water. Sprinkle some of the water all over your home, making sure you get the corners and windows.'

Colin sprinkled water all over the house, living room, kitchen, even the bathroom, and lastly the bedroom. He continued to read again.

'The Holy water will not work if you took it without permission from the church'

'Bloody hell why didn't you say that before I nicked it from St Anthony's. This damn water is all over the place, and now you're saying it won't work.'

Colin was getting madder and madder.

He read through the rest of the book; he was desperate to fight his demons.

'Aha! maybe this might work.'

He went into the kitchen; he was starting to get more and more desperate.

'Look at the mess in this place, water everywhere and it stinks of smoke. Where's the bloody salt?'

He found a packet of salt in a cupboard, and sprinkled it in the corners of the house and doorways. He then started banging the pots and pans together to scare away any demons.

'Go away! Mrs. Chan, leave me alone. Do not come to my house, Go! Go! You are not welcome in my house Go! Go! Away! Away! Away as far as you can.'

Colin was walking around the flat bagging the pots and pans. He felt a cold breeze behind him, and goose bumps around the back of his neck. He slowly turned around and walked into the bedroom. The wind was blowing through the window, and he looked straight across to Mrs Chan's window. He felt someone was watching him, but he couldn't see anything. Suddenly he heard a voice coming towards him on the wind.

'Colin, get the cat.'

'No way, you're not going to get my Lucifer Mrs. Chan. Over my dead body, or maybe your dead body. No way!'

Suddenly Colin noticed Mrs Chan staring at him from her window. She looked just as she did when she was alive. Colin couldn't move; he was frozen to the spot, and he felt he was about to pee his pants.

'Get the cat, get the cat,' said Mrs. Chan.

'No! No! you will not eat Lucifer.'

Mrs. Chan pointed her finger in the direction of Colin's bedside table. Colin turned around to look.

'Ah, so you want your golden cat. It's not my fault; I don't know how it got here. I don't want it; I think Lucifer took it from your house, but I returned it.'

Mrs Chan continued to point at the golden cat telling Colin to pick it up. He was starting to calm down a bit, and he picked up the cat.

'So, what do you want me to do with this? I can throw it right straight to your window if you want Mrs. Chan. Please don't make me return to your house again.'

Mrs. Chan was trying to communicate with Colin, by hand gestures. She was getting annoyed that Colin didn't understand her. She held up her right hand with the palm closed, and with a left-hand finger she poked it into the hole she'd made in her right hand. It looked like she was making the sexual gesture "you wanna fuck?"

'My god Mrs Chan, what are you suggesting?'

He eventually understood the message that she wanted him to turn the cat upside down and find the hole at the bottom. Colin found a little flap that unlocked, just like that on a coin bank.

'Aha, what have we here?'

Colin shook the cat and something rattled.

He opened the flap and a necklace fell out.

'Got it Mrs Chan,' but she had gone.

Later that night Colin went downstairs to Marco's shop. Mia opened the door on her way out.

'Oops Colin, sorry we closed now; it's almost midnight, and we no have leftovers; I gave all to stray cats at the back.'

Mia was smiling, making fun of Colin.

'No worries, Mia, I don't have an appetite for food tonight.'

'Oh, I sorry, me just joking Colin, are you ok?'

'It's ok, I just want to talk to Marco; is he still there. I tried his flat but there was no answer, so I figured out that he's still here.'

'Yup he's at the back emptying the bins; just go through. I go now before miss my bus; see you tomorrow, ciao.'

Colin opened the shop door.

'Sorry, we're closed,' called Marco.

'Oh it's you Colin my friend, come in come in, what do you want?'

'Just dropping by, no worries, I can wait. You just carry on with what you were doing, don't mind me.'

Colin sat down at a small table where the sanitiser gel and tissues were placed for the use of customers.

'Ok, I'm done here, do want to go to my flat or will we talk here?' said, Marco.

'We'll just talk here: I want to ask for some advice and get your thoughts.'

'Ok, I'm listening my friend. I'm always here for you Colin, you are my only friend in this country. So, go on, but don't ask me how business is going. Sales are not good nowadays, probably due to the cost of living, and not helped by Mia serving a customer with a deep-fried window washing sponge. You know people here; they talk and it's bad for business. But I'm sure it will be ok. Otherwise, I will close my shop and go back to Italy without accomplishing anything, no business, no house, not even a wife.'

Colin was giving Marco a dubious look.

'Oh, sorry my friend, you are here to talk about your problem; I just got carried away. So, go on, what advice do you want from me,' said Marco

'The thing is Marco, I'm in an extraordinary situation and I don't know what to do. I'm not crazy or anything, but I'm afraid of going to jail.' Colin suddenly stopped talking when Marco stood up, locked the door and looked outside through the blinds.

'What are you doing Marco?'

'I'm just checking to see if anyone's outside, I'm your friend Colin, but I do not want to be your accomplice. I want to go back to my country as an honourable man, perhaps without any accomplishment. But I do not want to go back there as a criminal and hide. Do you understand Colin, my friend?'

'Marco let me finish first.'

Marco sat down again opposite Colin.

'The other day you saw me in the house of Mrs. Chan.'

'Oh my god Colin, you murdered Mrs. Chan?'

'Nonoo, what makes you say that? I couldn't even hurt Lucifer, even if he scratches the hell out of me most of the time.'

'So, you accidentally killed Mrs. Chan, that's

why you went to her house that day? You were trying to remove any evidence. You should've asked for my help, Colin, we could have done it differently. But by pushing her on the stairs you may have left some evidence. We have another Italian way of killing someone without evidence.' Marco was leaning towards Colin and whispering.

'No Marco, I didn't kill anyone, I didn't kill Mrs. Chan or push her down the stairs.'

Colin was getting frustrated; he was standing up and walking around the shop.

'Ok, so what were you doing in Mrs. Chan's flat?'

'I was returning something that belongs to her. I don't even know when and how her golden cat figurine ended up in my flat. That was the day that Mrs. Chan was found dead on the stairs. It must have been Lucifer who took it. But I got it into my head that maybe the police would think I'd been in her flat after she died, and perhaps I had something to do with her death. And she once told me if she caught Lucifer in her flat, she would kill both of us. I just panicked and wanted to put the golden cat back where it belonged.'

'Well, that's Mrs. Chan. She also threatened to report me to the Food Safety and Hygiene department at the Council office, if I don't cook her fish in fresh oil. I wonder how she knew that I re-use my cooking oil twenty-three times. I don't want to waste money on cooking oil; you know what I mean Colin, business is business.'

'Listen Marco, I don't want to tell you the whole situation, because you'll think I'm crazy or losing my mind. Anyway, I put the golden cat back inside Mrs. Chan's flat, and this morning, when I woke up, it was back again on my bedside table. Now, I don't know if that bloody Lucifer maybe brought it back again; I just don't understand it. I discovered that the cat was hollow, and it could be opened at the bottom. When I opened it, a necklace fell out. Now, this is the spooky part. I met Mrs Chan's daughter and I'm doing the funeral service for her mother.

'You're joking Colin. How did that happen? I mean, how did the necklace get inside the cat?'

Colin was looking at Marco wondering why he was being so stupid.

'Are you listening to me, Marco? It's not about how the necklace got inside the cat, it's about the coincidence of me meeting Mrs Chan's daughter, and doing my first funeral service as a celebrant.'

Marco's eyes grew bigger.

'You mean to say that you kill Mrs. Chan to get your first celebrant job?'

'Marco, this is very frustrating talking to you. You're being ridiculous; let's just forget it.'

'Colin, I understand, you said coincidence, yes, that's it. Coincidence, what's wrong with coincidence?

'Her daughter doesn't know that I know her

mother, and she has told me the whole life story of her mother. And she also talked about the necklace that her mother gave her. The coincidence is - I found the necklace. The problem is - should I give it to her, and come clean about me knowing Mrs Chan? And don't ask me why I didn't do that in the first place. I can't get inside Mrs. Chan's flat anymore to put the cat and the necklace back. The police have locked up the flat and even the kitchen window is completely locked.'

'If I were you Colin, I would just keep the cat and the necklace. I mean, nobody knows right? The Police will also think that you had something to do with Mrs. Chan's death, so keep your mouth shut. No evidence, no one will go to jail, and everybody will be happy.'

'I think you're right Marco. Let's keep these things between the two of us.'

'What things, we never talk Colin; you were never here. Now, let me close the shop.'

Colin stood up and was about to leave the shop.

'What were you saying about the Italian way of killing someone, Marco?'

'Huh, oh that, have you seen the movie The Godfather?

Colin nodded his head; he knew what Marco was talking about.

'I need to go and start writing the eulogy for Mrs. Chan. Don't forget to attend the funeral, and wear a suit that doesn't smell of fish n chips, ok?'

CHAPTER EIGHT

Goodbye Mrs. Chan

The day of the funeral came around and Colin was very much aware that it is his first service. He was in the toilet of the crematorium alone. Standing in front of the mirror looking at himself, and not sure if he can do it. He started to have a panic attack, sweating with nervousness, and practicing his speech. Colin could feel a cold wind coming from a small window in the toilet. Suddenly one of the cubicles unlocked, and someone flushed the toilet. Colin had been sure that he was alone in there.

'Hello, who's there? Come out whoever you are.'

Colin thought that someone was going to attack him. The door of the cubicle suddenly swung open.

'What the fuck!'

Colin came face to face with Kevin, the crematorium technician.

'What the fuck are you doing there Kevin, you scared the shit out of me. I was sure I was in here on my own.

'Well, you didn't have to scare the shit out of

me, I managed that on my own as you can probably smell. I was here before you, and I was just sitting there listening while you practiced your speech.'

Kevin was washing his hands.

'I don't know if I can do this Kevin. You know this is my first work as a celebrant; I don't want anybody to notice that. And I'm not sure what I'm doing.'

'Relax, I've seen and heard a lot of Celebrants and most of them are a lot worse than you, from what I've just heard. Just kidding Colin; but seriously, you are better than most. And the more you do it, the more relaxed you will be. So, get yourself out there, I think the service is about to start.'

Colin decided to walk behind the coffin as the family carried it in. He caught the smell of something that was new to him.

'Oh god, that must be the smell of the body decomposing' he thought.

He watched the six members of the family carrying the coffin and trying not to trip over each other's feet.

'What if they drop it, he thought. Would the body roll across the floor?'

He could smell alcohol.

'Oh fuck, at least one of these guys has been to the pub and had a good drink. They are going to drop it, and I'm not helping them pick up the body and put it back in the box.'

Colin was trying to push these bad thoughts out of his mind.

The family with the help of the Funeral Director rolled the coffin onto the catafalque. When Colin first heard this word from a Funeral Director, he thought he said "catapult".

He wondered if this would catapult the coffin into the fiery furnace. This thought made him smile and relax a bit.

Colin stepped up to the lectern and looked out at the chapel full of mourners. He wasn't expecting so many people.

'Where did they all come from,' he thought. 'Mrs Chan was a grumpy old so and so and she didn't seem to have any friends.'

Mr and Mrs Daforth were sitting on the front pew along with their daughter Irene. Irene gave Colin a sad smile.

Colin started to speak; he was still nervous.
'Good morning, everyone. Sorry, sorry, good afternoon,' he stuttered. 'Eh, erm.'

He suddenly heard a familiar voice inside his head, it was Mrs Chan.

'Come on fool, get on with it. All you need to do is read my eulogy. Although some of it is rubbish that my daughter told you.'

Colin read his introduction and started reading the eulogy. He covered the life of Mrs. Chan from when she was a child to an adolescent, becoming a single mother to Lina, and all the ups and down she experienced. Her favourite food, her favourite music and her favourite books.

Colin then introduced Lina who had agreed to speak.

'I would like to ask Lina, Mrs. Chan's daughter to say a few words about her mother.' Colin stepped away from the lectern allowing Lina to speak.

'Ma, there are so many things I want to say to you that I wish I could have told you when you were still with me. I am not blaming you for anything, I do understand what you feel and I know the fear inside of you. You were a great mother, and you just wanted the best for me all the time. All your life is about me, I wouldn't be here if not for your guidance. You also have a habit of helping others secretly, you were quick to drop what you were doing and help someone in need in a matter of seconds. Selflessness was a trait that reflected everything you were about. I wish you could still be here with us, to share the laughter, success, and pain we always had, Ma, wherever you are. I'm sorry for my shortcomings, and soon we will meet again.'

Colin was touched by Lina's short speech, and he looked out at the people, expecting to see Mrs Chan. And there she was, at the end of a row of seats. She was listening to every word her daughter said about her. She was smiling and looked at peace as she slowly walked toward the door at the back of the chapel. She turned and mouthed.

'Thank you to Colin.'

The Funeral Director was standing off to the side and he whispered, 'Colin, Colin it's your turn.'

'Thank you, Lina, for your lovely words. I would now like to conclude this ceremony.

Colin finalised the service and thanked everyone on behalf of the family for coming.

Outside the crematorium everyone was chatting and saying their goodbyes. Colin and Marco were standing at the door of the crematorium, watching everyone.

The Funeral Director tapped Colin on the shoulder.

'Colin, that was an exceptional service. We'll definitely contact for future services.'

'Thank you so much, it was my pleasure. Can I ask why you chose me for Mrs. Chan's funeral service? I haven't had the chance to visit your Funeral Service before; who referred me to your company?' Colin inquired.

'It was Mrs. Chan herself. She came to our office with her funeral plans and provided us with your business card. She insisted that no one else but you should conduct her service, speaking highly of you as the best Celebrant she's known. I believe her now. Good luck, Colin. See you later, bye.'

A sudden realization struck Colin. He remembered encountering Mrs. Chan on the stairs of his flat, and dropping his bag of business cards. She nearly tripped over it and had grumbled at him.

'Out of my way, you silly man,' she scolded, waving her walking stick.

'And stop dumping your rubbish all over the stairs.'

'Mrs. Chan, that's not fair; come on, at least lend a hand' Colin had appealed, gathering the cards carefully.

'Help yourself, you idiot!' she retorted.

Yet, Colin recalled, that despite not assisting, she had bent down and picked up a card. At the time, he assumed she'd throw it away, but it seemed she had kept it. Colin smiled, realizing that perhaps Mrs. Chan wasn't such a bad neighbour after all.

'I told you my friend that you could do it. That's an easy job, maybe you can teach me someday when I retire from my shop. I want to become a celebrant also.' said Marco.

'It's easy for you to say, Marco, I almost shit myself when I saw all those people looking at me. I wasn't expecting that so many people would show up today. You know how grumpy and unfriendly Mrs Chan was.'

Lina and Henry Daforth approached Colin.

'Thank you very much for making a wonderful eulogy for my mother,' said Lina. I'm sure wherever she is now she would be delighted, proud and honoured, and would thank you also.'

'And I'm sure, Lina, that she would be very happy and moved by your kind words.'

Colin shook hands with Lina and Henry.

Marco stepped forward.

'My condolences Mr and Mrs Daforth; my name is Marco and I'm one of your mother's neighbours.'

He shook hands with Henry and Lina.

'Nice to meet you Marco,' said Henry, 'and thank you for coming. And we also thank you for all the information and helping the police investigating her death. There is nothing to worry about now. The case is closed; it was an accident. The police showed us the video from the CCTV camera in the stairs at the flats. It clearly shows she had an accident and fell down the stairs.'

Marco was smiling at Henry.

'What is it, why are you smiling,' asked Henry.

'It's nothing, I'm just glad that everything is

fine, no murder, no robbery, no one going to jail. Good stuff eh. I mean my condolences, got to go, bye.'

Marco hurriedly walked to the car park where Colin was waiting for him in the car.

'Colin, good news my friend, you are not going to jail.'

'Lower your voice, Marco, what are you talking about.'

Colin was still nervous and looking around from inside the car.

'Colin, the investigation of Mrs. Chan's death is closed, we are free my friend. The husband told me that they'd seen the CCTV video from the camera on the stairs. They saw Mrs Chan trip over her big shopping bag, flip over and bang her head. No one hit her on the head, it was an accident. Isn't that good news Colin?'

Colin couldn't say a word and still looked worried.

'Why my friend are you still looking worried. You and I are not going to jail.'

'Well, I don't think there was any chance of you going to jail Marco. Not unless she passed out after eating some of your fish n chips cooked in old rotten oil. Why didn't you tell me before, that there's a CCTV camera on those stairs.'

'Did you not notice the camera, said Marco.

It's been there since Mrs Chan moved in. In fact, she put up most of the money to have it installed.'

'Well, I may not be charged with murder, but I will be charged with robbery. And remember the day I broke into her flat to take back the golden Cat. What if someone saw me - fuck! fuck!'

'Well, at least you'll not be in jail for a long time. I mean, you only get 2 to 3 years for burglary.'

They were both quiet and not talking to each other.

'I have an idea, Colin, trust me.'

A few days later, Lina Daforth answered her front door to a postman.

'Are you Mrs. Lina Daforth?' said the postman.

'Yes.'

'Package for you.'

The postman handed over the package and immediately walked away.

'Wait, do I need to sign or anything?'

'Em, nope it's ok that's an old package; sorry for the delay, bye.'

Lina was confused, and she felt a bit strange. She thought she had seen the Postman before. She took the parcel into the kitchen and opened it on the worktop.

'Oh, my goodness, it's the golden cat and mum's necklace. Where did this come from?' She started to cry.

Around the corner from the Daforth's house, the postman climbed into a car.

'Are you sure they didn't recognize you, Marco?

Marco took off his sunglass and Royal Mail baseball cap.

'Yes Colin; I'm good at working incognito. Nobody recognised me. Now, you owe me £50. I just borrowed this Posty uniform from my friend, and I need to give him something,' said Marco.

Colin started the engine.

CHAPTER NINE

New Neighbour

Colin pressed the doorbell and Mia opened the door with a big smile. There was an even bigger smile when she saw the bunch of flowers in front of her.

'Hi, I hope I'm not late for the party.'

Colin handed the flowers to Mia.

'You no have to buy me flowers Colin, Grazie, for your thoughts. And this wine is too much. Come in, the party is just about to start.'

'It's a British tradition to bring a new neighbour a small gift. Well, I'm not sure if people still do it nowadays. I'm a bit old fashioned.'

Colin was looking around Mia's flat. It seemed that everything was in place, He noticed that she had a lot of old paintings, which looked expensive. Some of them looked familiar.

'Do you like a paintings, Colin?

'Naah, I'm not into art but my grandma used to take me to art galleries, she liked to paint. Which reminds me; she has a friend in Cornwall and they painted together. Maybe I should visit her someday and check if she has any of my gran's paintings. I think she kept them in her house, and I forgot to tell her that Gran passed away. '

'Well, I no been to Cornwall before; maybe I go with you Colin if you visit her someday.'

'Yeah, I would love that, let's see what tomorrow brings.'

Colin picked up a big painting from the floor and admired the colours and its beauty.'

'Don't stare too long at that painting Colin, it's a no real'.

'Well, it doesn't matter if it's real or not, I don't even know who painted it, but it looks familiar to me.'

He hung the painting above the fireplace.

Mia tapped his shoulder.

'That's perfect Colin, now help me move the sofa right there in the corner, I want to sit beside the window.'

'You're lucky to grab Mrs. Chan's flat, there were a lot of people inquiring about it. I thought that Mrs. Chan owned it, but I was wrong she was just renting it.'

Mia was in the kitchen putting the flowers in a vase.

'Are you sure you want to do this Colin? I really no want to bother you if you are busy with your celebrant thing. I can manage here, besides my furniture arrived this morning and have help of…' The doorbell rang again.

'Mi scusi, Colin.'

'Are you expecting someone? I thought it was just the two of us at this party.

'No, no, Ali he come. He give me help and give me old furniture and things for the kitchen. I was gonna to look in the charity shops, but no need now.'

Colin was a bit disappointed when he saw Ali come in. He was hoping to be alone with Mia, help her clean the flat and arrange the furniture.

'Hello my friend, Colin, nice to see you here. I brought some Chinese takeaway for lunch for two. I wasn't expecting that Mia and I have company. But I'm sure the food is enough for the three of us, I'm not that hungry.

'I so thank you again for everything Ali,' said Mia. 'All these things that you give me, the furniture, kitchen stuff, and now the free food. I not know how to thank you enough.'

'Ah, no worries, anything for you Mia, no problem, I will always be around to help. If you need any help, I'll be here as soon as I can. Not like some people who show up when the work is finished.' He was grinning at Colin, who was becoming irritated.

'Well, let's start the party,' said Colin. Where do you want me to start cleaning Mia? I think we should divide up the jobs that need done. Ali, you clean the toilet, and I will start painting the bedroom with Mia.' He handed a toilet brush to Ali.

Colin and Mia started painting the bedroom.

'Are you happy living here on your own Mia? I don't mean to be disrespectful, but the rent of this flat is more expensive than mine. It's a bit bigger of course, but are you sure you can manage?'

'No worry about me Colin; Marco pay my two months deposit and two months advance, so everything is okay. And I still have the savings to pay my rent for another six months. By that time maybe I meet millionaire who pay for my upkeep.' Mia was smiling.

At lunchtime the three of them ate in the kitchen, sharing the Chinese takeaway that Ali brought in. Most of the time Ali was monopolising the conversation; every time Colin started to say something Ali interrupted him.

'Can you smell Mrs. Chan,' said Ali. 'I feel that she's still in this house roaming around. Are you sure Mia it's ok for you to be alone, I mean if you want some company, especially at night I can come round easily you know that my shop is just around the corner.'

'Don't be daft Ali of course you can smell Mrs. Chan, we're eating Chinese food here. Please don't put crazy stuff in Mia's brain. I'm sure she will be ok here.'

It was late afternoon, when they finished cleaning and painting the entire flat and Mia, was very pleased with her new home.

'Well, that's it, thank you both for help me out, I no do it alone. So, you please accept my dinner invitation for tomorrow night. That is if you no busy with your work. Please say yes; it's for me to pay, and I will be very sad if you turn me down.'

Ali responded right away.

'Just like I said Mia, anything for you I will always be around, and I will not be late tomorrow night.'

He gave a disdainful look at Colin.

'No worries, Mia, I will be there also. I have some work during the day but will catch up with you later, and I will not be late.' said Colin.

The following day Colin was driving his old Volvo in an expensive residential area of the city. He was trying to find the address of his next client and muttering to himself.

'What do these people do that live in houses like these, and where the fuck is number 68? They're all big houses but you can hardly see the house numbers. And look at the cars in the driveways - Range Rovers, Jaguars, Ferraris, and two or three cars at each house.'

He spotted the number, and drove into the driveway of a big Victorian house; the car tyres crunching on the gravel. There was an elderly woman waiting at the door.

'This must be the mother of the deceased,' he thought. He looked at his watch to check if he was late.

'Good, right-on time.'

He slammed the door of his car but forgot to close the car window at the back. He tried to open the driver's door but the door was fighting back.

'C'mon, don't give me a hard time, why are you stuck up again.'

'Don't worry about that dear, I'm sure no one will bother to steal something from your car it's safe here.'

'I'm not worried about the neighbourhood it's the rain that I'm worried about. The last time I left the window open, I could see fishes swimming inside my car. Hi, I'm Colin Bott, you must be Mrs. Jones.' He reached for her hand.

'Yes, I'm Fiona Jones; please come in. My husband is in his office. I was worried that you would have a hard time finding our house because of the tall trees and bushes. I was telling Robert my husband to arrange for it to be trimmed, but he is bothered about the cost, if you know what I mean.'

Colin reluctantly agreed to what she was saying, but to his mind he couldn't understand why they would be bothered about the cost. With that big house and two luxury cars parked in their driveway, there's no way that they should be bothered about money.

'Yeah, I know; but if you want a cheap hedge cutter guy, I can come back and trim your bush. I mean your garden bushes, for a very cheap price.'

Mrs Jones didn't seem to understand what Colin was saying, but she laughed anyway.

'Hahaha, you have a good sense of humour Colin, I like you already.'

She opened the door, led Colin up the long hallway, knocked on a door and went inside.

'Hello, darling this is Colin Bott; he's a celebrant and the Funeral Director sent him to do the funeral service for Michael. Have a seat, Colin.'

She pointed at one of the two sofas in the room. The man sitting at the desk didn't raise his head and carried on doing his paperwork.

'He'll be with us in a minute, would you like to have something to drink?' she whispered to Colin.

'Just water would be fine Fiona.'
'Ok, I will be right back.'

Colin cleared his throat trying to catch the attention of the man at the desk

'Sorry about that, I can't stop if I'm in the middle of something. I tend to forget, so I must write down all the important things before I do.'

'No problem, I do understand. I'm a busy person too, I'm Colin Bott.'

He reached out his hand but the man just waved and sat opposite Colin on the other sofa.

'I'm Robert Jones, you can call me Robert. I will be direct and honest with you Colin; I do not want to get involved with this funeral thing. Don't get me wrong, but I don't think I am the right person to give you information about Michael. My son and I had our differences; I haven't spoken to him for almost two years now. I'm not sure if I will be there on the day of the funeral. But I have written some information about him, about his childhood. Maybe you can use it for his eulogy; other than that, I can't share any more of my thoughts about him.'

Fiona Jones arrived with a cup of coffee and a bottled of water.

Robert Jones stood up.

'Ok, I will leave the two of you alone, I need to do some errands. Fiona, can you give Colin the paper that I've written, it's inside the top drawer of my desk. Good to meet you Colin, now if you excuse me.'

'Can you stay for a minute at least just to listen to our conversation Robert?' Pleaded his wife.

He gave her a dismissive look and left the room. Fiona was embarrassed and sat down with Colin.

'Ok, let's just start Colin, just tell me what

you need and I will give you all the information regarding my son.'

'The funeral will be next week; I was informed by the funeral director about the music that will be used for the opening and the end. Please can you check if everything here in the form is correct Fiona.'

After an hour of conversation, Colin managed to get all the information he needed to write a eulogy about Michael's life, but something was not quite right.

'If you don't mind Fiona, you never mentioned anything about Michael's present life it's all about his childhood and education. That's okay, but do you not want me to mention more about his current life at least his last two years?

'I know what you mean Colin, I think my husband told you about our relationship with Michael, we never spoke to him well, but that is not quite true. I've been in contact with my son even though I'm not allowed to by my husband, but I'm a mother. I maybe not be the right person to talk about Michael's life, but I will give you Stephen's number and address. He is the right person to talk to, regarding Michael's life.'

Fiona wrote the address on a piece of paper, and handed it over along with the paper that her husband left in his desk drawer.

'Well, that's about it Mrs. Jones, I should probably go now. And I will visit Stephen and get more information about your son. Thank you and nice meeting you.'

They both walk along the hallway.

'I apologise for my husband's behaviour. He still in shock about Michael's death, and there are things that you wouldn't understand now. I hope it will make things easier for you after you meet Stephen.'

'No problem, Mrs. Jones I will visit Stephen, and see you at the funeral service.'

Colin set out for his date with Mia at the pub.

When he arrived, he saw Mia sitting in the corner; she waved and smiled at Colin. He was happy to see her - alone. Just as he was about to sit down beside her, Ali arrived holding a drink for Mia and a pint of beer for himself.

'Well, well, late again Colin, eh! So, what's your excuses this time. Traffic, or your old car won't start, or maybe you were avoiding paying for our drinks eh!'

Colin ignored him.

'I'm sorry Mia. No, there was no traffic problems along the way because I decided not to bring my car. It's too hard to park in this area. And another thing, I wasn't avoiding paying for drinks. In fact, you drink as many beers as you like Ali and I will pay for them, because I had another job today. This was the reason I was a little bit late. I have a proper job Ali, and I'm earning money from my job, thank you very much.'

Colin was trying to hide his annoyance with Ali.

'No problem, Colin; we come here 5 mins ago, you no miss a thing. Ali no drive his car so we take the train. So, how's your day been, you happy,' said Mia.

'Not really, happy, happy, just a bit more comfortable because this is my second funeral service, and I think I'm getting used to it. I'm just hoping it will continue and I get more jobs in the future; you know what I mean.'

'I don't think you will have more job as a celebrant Colin, 'I've seen other celebrants before and they know how to crack a joke, and always be the life and soul of the party. You're more of a boring type of a person.' Ali's beer spilled all over his shirt while he was talking.

'And why would I need to crack jokes being a celebrant, Ali?

'Well, is that not what a celebrant is for? You're the one who makes joke in the party or in the club. You're celebrating, and you go to birthdays, wedding anniversaries and shit stuff like that? Am I right?'

Mia and Colin were laughing

'Ali, Colin is different celebrant than what you talk about. You just silly. I no know about Colin job, but it's about funerals like a priest,' said Mia.

Colin whispered in Mia's ear.

'Don't worry Mia, you don't need to explain to Ali, his brain can't understand very much.'

'I heard that Colin, I'm not that stupid you know. Anyway, can we start our dinner. Is this self-service or will someone take our order, I'm starving.'

Mia signalled to one of the waitresses.

'Are you ready to order now?' The pretty blond waitress started tapping details into her tablet while Ali was ogling her bottom. Colin noticed and felt embarrassed; he kicked Ali under the table.

'Oi,' why are you kicking me?

'Ok, boys,' said Mia. You have what you want, no worries; it's a my treat for helping me yesterday.'

'Thank you, Mia. You know I will always be here to help you. I'll have fish and chips I'm not that hungry anyway.' Ali was leering at Mia.

Colin had to have his say.

'You don't need to worry Mia, you know you can always count on me, and since I now have another job, let me pay for tonight. Anyway, this is the first time that we've had dinner together. It would be nice if it was just the two of us, of course. No offense Ali, but three's a crowd. And I hope you understand; after all, who wouldn't want to be alone with Mia right?'

'No, no, Colin, I not allow you pay for the dinner it's for me, like I promise.'

'Let him be Mia, if Colin wants to be generous tonight, then let it be, He has even insisted that we can drink as many beers as we want. I've known this guy for years now, and he is not a generous guy. But if he insists on something like this, then we should be kind enough to accept his generosity. I'm starting to feel a bit hungry now; excuse me miss beautiful waitress, what is your special today?'

'Well Sir, you should try our Beef Wellington. It is made with fillet steak coated with pâté and wrapped in puff pastry, and then baked.

'That sounds delicious to me, I'll have that. What about you Mia? Perhaps you should also try this. After all, this is Colin's treat for his second job.'

'I have carbonara thank you, what about you Colin?' said Mia

Colin was starting to get irritated with Ali. He casually checked the prices on the menu. Beef Wellington cost £35 and Carbonara £18. He was starting to think that this bill will melt his credit card, especially with desserts and drinks. He was starting to regret opening his big mouth, and didn't hear Mia speaking to him.

'What, what's that Mia? I'm not really

hungry. I think I'll just have a starter; I had quite a lot at lunchtime.'

'So, what kind of starter would you like,' said the smiling waitress,' pointing to the menu.

'Just give me the cheapest, I mean the tastiest.'

The waitress was still smiling at Colin and starting to feel a bit sorry for him.

'I tell you what sir, if you are not hungry, why don't I give you a small plate, and you can help yourself to our salad bar. It's free,' she whispered and winked at Colin.

After a short wait, the waitress brought the beef wellington for Ali and the pasta dish for Mia.

Colin was looking at the food and his stomach was starting to rumble. He hadn't in fact had much for his lunch, only a small sandwich. And now the sight of Ali wolfing down his meal, grunting like a pig in a trough, was really starting to annoy him.

'I hope you choke you fucker,' he thought.

Colin suddenly heard a voice behind him.

'Did you know that people who eat their food too quickly are more likely to suffer from gastroesophageal reflux disease. This occurs when stomach acids wash up into the oesophagus and cause symptoms such as chest pain and heartburn.'

'What; who said that?'

Colin whirled around to see where this voice was coming from, but there was no one there.

'Colin! Help! Ali he choking!'

Mia was shouting and dragging Colin from his thoughts.

Ali *was* choking and having a hard time to breath. People in the restaurant were looking on, and that was all they were doing. The manager rushed over asking everyone if there was a doctor in the restaurant.

Colin heard the voice from behind again.

'You need to help him.'

'Let's give him a couple of minutes, said Colin.'

He was quite enjoying watching Ali suffer. But Mia started shouting in panic.

'Do something Colin, he's going to choke to death.'

Colin stood up, and he heard the voice again.

'Stand behind the person who's choking. Place your arms around their waist and bend them forward. Clench your fist and place it right above their belly button. Put your other hand on top of your fist and pull sharply inwards and upwards. Repeat this movement up to 5 times.'

Colin followed the instruction from the mysterious voice.

'C'mon you bastard, don't die on me. If you die, I'll take your credit card to pay the bill, you stupid idiot!'

That seemed to provoke a reaction from Ali. All of a sudden, he spat out a lump of steak straight into the wine glass of a man at the next table, who was holding it in his hand.

The manager spotted it and grabbed the glass from the astonished man's hand.

'I will get you another glass of wine sir, on the house.'

Ali was recovering and the people in the restaurant started applauding Colin.

The manager was obviously concerned; he didn't like to think a customer would choke on the food they served in his restaurant, and he wanted to be sure no one would sue him.

'Gentlemen and madam, I do apologise for this situation. We will take care of your bill this evening. Please feel free to order whatever you wish. We wouldn't like to think you would give us a bad review over this incident.'

'Thank you very much, said Colin.

'Perhaps the fillet steak was a little difficult to chew. Are you sure it was fillet steak in your beef wellington? That is usually so tender that it melts in your mouth. But we appreciate your generosity.

And all this drama and exercise has made my appetite return. Can I have a look at the menu again, perhaps I will have steak au poivre and check out the fillet steak for myself. And perhaps a bottle of Saint Emilion Grand Cru to wash it down. We wouldn't me to choke on the steak, would we?'

'Certainly sir. Your waitress, Marie, will help you now.'

The manager walked away not looking happy at what he had committed to.

Colin had never tried St Emillion wine, but he knew it was much better that the cheap plonk he was used to buying.

'I thought you not hungry,' said Mia.

'I think it was probably the stress and rush of adrenaline into my system that brought back my appetite.

'And what about you Miss, would you like a dessert.? Said Marie.

'No, thank you very much.'

Ali was starting to recover.

'Perhaps I could have the beef wellington again and enjoy my steak for the second time.'

'Oh, I think you should try our salmon, Sir, we don't want another battle with the steak for tonight.'

Mia was smiling at Colin.

'Why are you looking at me like that Mia?'

'Well for a start, I am most impress how you

saved our friend Ali from the horrendous accident that tried to kill him. How you know what to do, and speaking all the instructions and counting as you did it. With all the instructions you say, I think you were giving us a lecture. You knew what you do and give us commentary at the same time. I am impressed medico Colin. Let us have drunk for your hero act my friend. And Ali, you no want to thank Colin for saving your life?'

Ali wasn't enjoying all the attention Colin was receiving.

'Well, my friend I don't know if it was heroic saving a choking person, but I salute you for saving my life, according to Mia.'

They raised their glass, but Colin was a bit apprehensive. He was thinking, 'Yeah, I did save Ali from choking but where did that voice come from, telling me what to do, and why was I speaking the instructions out loud. Hey, I'll just enjoy the moment.'

It was almost midnight when they left the restaurant. Ali had obviously drunk too much. He was staggering and slurring his words. The free food and drink was something he couldn't refuse. But the last large Drambuie had really hit him.

'I think we should go home now Ali; you've had a lot to drink and your mother will not be happy. You promised her that you wouldn't be late. And listen; I thought your religion didn't allow the drinking of alcohol. You're in big shit pal.' Said Colin. And he looked at Mia.

'I think we should call a taxi and send him home.'

'Are you sure Colin, we can take the train.'

She was worried about Ali.

'I don't think it's a good idea, Mia. The last time Ali and I were drunk he started to vomit inside the train. They threw us off the train at the next station, and we nearly spent the night in jail. Ali was insulting the Guard on the train and the Railway Police were called. It's much better if the taxi driver takes him home. Don't worry I have his wallet with me and will pay for his journey in advance. It'll save him getting ripped off or robbed.'

Colin had a big smile.

CHAPTER TEN

Hey Mikey

Once they arranged for Ali to take a taxi home, Mia and Colin strolled towards the train station, finally allowing Colin a moment alone with her. He felt elated just being in her company, even if at times he struggled to grasp her words. Whether it was her accent or her grammar, it didn't matter to Colin. Each syllable that flowed from Mia's lips sounded delightful to him. Her luscious lips and captivating wide eyes, coupled with her exotic Italian appearance, held Colin's attention every passing minute. As he listened to her tales and chuckled along, he found himself feeling akin to a schoolboy, infatuated with an alluring teacher. Everything about Mia seemed extraordinary to Colin.

'Why did you decide to live in the UK Mia? Italy is a much better country in terms of weather; here it's always gloomy and rainy.'

'I just wanted to be independent, away from my father. You know what Italian families are like, we stick together even if we are grown up or even have our own family. Do not get me wrong, and think me a bad person. I love my family very much, but I want my freedom. It is very complicated Colin you will no understand, I'm not what you think I am.'

'Well, as long as you are not some kind of criminal or vampire, or you are hiding from someone that you owe a lot of money. Wait! Is that the reason why you want to marry a rich man, because you scam someone from your own country?'

'Hahahhaha, you so funny Colin, why would I do that, I no need to scam money from other people.'

'Well, a beautiful girl like you could easily fool any man you wanted.'

'Is that so, Colin? So, you mean to say that I could a fool you?'

He was blushing, he didn't know how to respond.

'Anyway, Colin, tell me about your childhood.'

'There's not much to tell. Being the only child, there weren't many antics or sibling teasing around the house. Unfortunately, my parents passed away when I was seven. These aren't movie scripts, by the way; they're real stories. But I'm proud of my parents; even in their passing, they quietly donated their organs, lungs, heart, and more to the community as their final act of love.'

'One day, I returned home and the fire alarm was blaring through the house. I found my mum and dad on the sofa, beside each other—my mum still in her hair rollers, and my dad in his pyjamas. They appeared as if peacefully asleep, holding hands, wearing faint smiles, like they had found solace together. The house was filled with cannabis smoke due to the fact that they smoked it all the time. I turned off the alarm, and that was the last time I saw them.

As Mia began to speak again, Colin gently placed his palm over her mouth.

'Then came the funeral—everything seemed meticulously planned. A multitude of mourners, weeping and wailing. But I didn't recognise a single one of them; they were all distant relatives and friends of my parents. Each person tossed some dirt onto the coffin; my Gran said it was tradition. Among the people who were there, there was a lot of cursing. One man said,

'You crook, you still owe me money; we'll settle this when we meet again.'

Another added, 'Good riddance, Conrad! Now that you're six feet under, you can't mess around with our wives.'

'Everyone had something to say; I couldn't grasp half of it. Gran covered my ears, perhaps shielding me from what was being said.

'So, how your parents pass away?' Mia asked. 'Was it the cannabis?'

'They both succumbed to lung cancer. My dad also battled an illness that caused him to vomit blood; something to do with his stomach. But that was them—even in sickness, they cared deeply for the village and its people. To this day, I'm proud of them.'

Mia was sad listening to his story.

'Come on, Mia, we can't afford to miss our train.'

As they waited for the train, Colin noticed a young man on his phone, he appeared to be upset. He was engaged in what seemed like an argument, while pacing back and forth. Suddenly, he stumbled and fell onto the railway tracks. Colin rushed towards him, lost his balance, and almost fell onto the train tracks himself. Mia grabbed Colin and pulled him to the side just as a train pulled in.

'What you thinking, Colin? Are you outa your mind? You nearly killed yourself'

'What? What did I do? Didn't you see that man? He was almost hit by the train, or at least I think he was.'

'What man? It was you that nearly hit the train! Maybe you try hurt yourself because of your painful stories about your madre e padre? This doesn't make sense. Colin, look at me, are you okay?'

Colin felt a bit disoriented and confused. He walked up and down, looking around and holding his head.

'Seriously, Mia, did you not see that guy who

fell on the train lines or jumped trying to kill himself?'

'Colin, we go home. You need to rest. There's nobody else around here, just us. It's alright, relax. We take a bus; we missed our train, and it's safer for you.'

Mia tried to calm him down.

Later the night, Colin found himself drenched in sweat; his heart was racing as if it might cease beating. He wanted to escape from this place, but despite his efforts to run, his legs wouldn't work and he found himself in a village which was eerily deserted. He knocked on doors, pleading for help, but no one bothered to answer.

'Help! Is anyone there? Please, I don't know where I am! Hello!'

He cried out repeatedly, relentless in his knocking until he reached the dead-end of the road. To his horror, there was a cemetery in front of him. A chill swept over him, leaving him trembling and terrified.

He spotted Lucifer standing at the cemetery gate. As the gate creaked open, Lucifer began to walk into the darkness.

'Luci... Luci, we can't go there.'

Colin pleaded.

'Damn it! His voice was rising in panic.
'Damn it!'

The ground began to tremble, and to Colin's horror, the dead started emerging from their graves.

'Noooo!' he screamed in terror.

Colin sprinted away, chased by the undead and other unidentifiable things. Suddenly, he jolted awake, still shouting and caught in the throes of his nightmare.

The next morning Colin shuffled about like a zombie as he began his morning rituals, kicking off with a lengthy trip to the bathroom and a thorough face wash in cold water.

'That's it, no more heavy drinking, even if it is on the house. Bloody headache... Where's the paracetamol?'

He grumbled, swiftly downing a couple of tablets to ease the pain. Sipping tap water, he peered at his reflection in the mirror.

'You're still a looker, Colin, even when you feel rubbish. Keep telling yourself that,' he muttered, attempting to boost his spirits. He prepared his breakfast, yawning his head off, boiled some water for coffee, popped some bread in the toaster. And poured some cereal into a bowl. Spreading some butter and jam on his toast, he hummed a tune. He was trying to push away the headache rather than give it any attention. He spread out the newspaper on the table.

'What's my horoscope for today? Here we go, do not worry today, for tomorrow is another day. What a load of rubbish—of course, tomorrow is another day. Wait a minute, this is yesterday's paper! No wonder people are not buying newspapers as often as they used to.'

Colin sat, sipping his coffee and munching on his toast. He was reading about a man who was tragically hit by a train.

'Another idiot jumping in front of a train to end it all... What a terrible choice for suicide. I'd rather drink poison or hold my breath for 15 minutes. That's my kind of exit. What a moron.' He muttered to himself.

As he reached for the milk to pour it over his cereal, the bowl moved, and the milk ended up on the table.

'What the heck!'

Colin jumped up from the table to find a cloth to wipe up the milk which was now on the floor. Lucifer had beaten him to it, and was lapping up the milk. Colin was on his knees wiping up the milk under the table when he spotted shiny black shoes with feet in them. Slowly, he inched backward and cautiously peered over the table.

'Who are you. Calling me a moron?'

There was a man sitting at Colin's kitchen table.

'What the fuck!' Colin crawled backward, completely stunned to see this man in his kitchen. He froze, staring at the man.

'Stand up and sit at the table. It's okay. I won't bite.'

Colin did as he was told, he was in complete shock.

'Now sit and listen carefully, Colin.'

'Yeah, yeah, I'm listening until this dream's over. You can't hurt me; this is just a dream.'

Colin was rambling.
The man chuckled.

'Hahaha! I'm starting to like you, Colin. You're a funny guy, and I appreciate that.'

The man strolled around the table, examining Colin's flat.

'You live alone, Colin?'

'Yeah, well, not exactly. I have company—my cat, Luci! Puss, puss... Where are you, Luci? He must be around or maybe not. This is just a dream, so Lucifer isn't here.'

'I hope you're not referring to '*The* Lucifer.' I prefer being up here, not down there, if you catch my drift,' the man quipped.

'Can we fast-forward to the good part? I'm feeling queasy. These bizarre dreams aren't helping my headache. I should've taken four tablets, not two. Can I wake up now, please?' Colin pleaded.

The man sat beside Colin.

'Alright, let's start again. Read the newspaper aloud, as if I'm not here. Drink your coffee, and finish your toast.'

'You want me to read this newspaper?'

'Yeah, read it. It's yesterday's newspaper. Just read the headlines.'

'A woman was assaulted and nearly raped by three drunks last night. None of them succeeded, however, as she managed to capture them all. The three men complained to the police that they were the ones who were violated. They said they were only talking to the woman as she walked through the park alone. The next thing they remembered was waking up, naked, and tied to a tree. All three complained that their testicles felt as if an elephant had been dancing on them, and their chances of having children were now highly unlikely.'

Colin burst out laughing. But the man gave Colin a deadpan stare.

'Sorry, I thought it was funny. So, do you want me to continue?'

'Read the next page, Colin.'

'Alright, let's see... Oh, more bad news.'

Colin sighed.

'A devastating incident occurred at Whoopon train station last Friday involving a man found deceased. He had fallen onto the railway tracks in front of a train coming into the station. The police are currently investigating the matter, leaning towards the possibility of suicide. Although the exact cause remains unconfirmed. The family have been notified and have confirmed the body to be their 35-year-old son, Doctor Michael Jones. The funeral arrangements are being arranged for this week at the Crematorium.'

Colin suddenly recalled the man he witnessed at the station who he thought had leaped onto the rails.

'You know, I was there with a friend, and I saw another idiot jump. My friend didn't see a thing, maybe I'm hallucinating. You can't imagine how many crazies choose to end their lives using trains or buses. Think about the chaos and damage they cause, not to mention the horrific scenes of scattered guts and brains; it's just selfish.'

Noticing the man's silence, Colin slammed the newspaper down.

'FOR FUCK'S SAKE!'

Colin's eyes widened as he locked onto the corpse before him—a mangled head, a blood-soaked shirt, a face unrecognizable to anyone.

'Hey there, Colin. Nice to meet you,'

Colin realised he hadn't really looked at the man before now.

'You! You're the guy who leaped onto the train tracks. You're the one in the news?'

'Yep, that's me. Caught red-handed!'

Colin hastily stood, feeling panic surge through him. He grabbed a glass of water, gulping it down frantically, slapping his face, attempting to wash away this surreal situation.

'Come on, Colin, wake up! This can't be real. You're just dreaming, damn it, wake up!'

Michael, the corpse, handed Colin a face towel that he had soaked in cold water.

'Thank you.' He mumbled taking the towel and wiping his face. He glanced nervously at the figure in front of him.

'Stay away! I'll call the police. Back off, I swear, I'm losing my mind here!'

He clutched a bread knife, moving away from Michael's corpse.

'Colin, just calm down and listen, okay? First, you're not dreaming. Second, you can't kill me; I'm already dead. Third, no one will believe you. They'll think you're losing it, going cuckoo. So, sit there and let's be realistic.' Michael urged.

'Realistic? You call this realistic? I'm here talking to a bloody corpse, and you expect me to relax and just listen.'

'What's your choice, Colin? Do you want me to fade from your mind? Do you want me to leave? Believe me, I've tried, but somehow, I'm connected to you.'

'What? Are you saying I wasn't dreaming or going crazy or drunk last night when I saw a man jump? It was you?'

'Yeah, unfortunately. I can't go anywhere.'

'I need a strong pill. Maybe if I sleep again, things will return to normal.' Colin muttered.

'Colin, let's figure this out. Things happen for a reason. I think we can help each other here. I'm not a bad person, you know. You should thank me; because of me, you became a hero in the restaurant last night.

'What do you mean?'

Colin was bewildered, then suddenly realised that Michael's voice was the one guiding him with Ali choking.

'It was you, the voice telling me what to do when greedy Ali was choking.'

'Yup, it was me, and all I'm asking for is a thank you,' Michael replied.

'I'm sorry, I'm just confused about why this is happening to me. These past few months, some creepy, unimaginable things happened, and I can't explain it. I certainly don't want to talk about it to my friends. I don't want them to think I'm a lunatic. But I think it's getting worse now. Look at me, I'm talking to you, and talking to Mrs. Chan.'

'Whose Mrs. Chan?'

'Oh, she was my Chinese neighbour who

hated me. Anyway, I now just accept things as normal. I don't do drugs, not even marijuana anymore. I tried it once with my parents when I was five. Maybe my brain was messed up then.'

'I understand, Colin. I didn't have a happy childhood either. Everything was controlled by my dad. Everything was always supervised.'

After a brief moment of silence, Colin cautiously spoke.

'See, I think we can work things out. Figure out why we're connected here.'
'What's your name again?'
Colin asked.

'My name is Michael Jones, but you can call me Mikey.'
'And your parents are?'
'Robert and Fiona Jones.'
'I'm Colin Bott, I'm going to be the funeral Celebrant at your Service.'
'Nice meeting you, Colin Bott. Let's acknowledge that you and I are connected for a purpose.'

Michael extended his hand to Colin, who nervously waved back, still uneasy around the corpse. One of Michael's eyes fell into Colin's cereal, bobbing in the Weetabix milk.

'Oops, my apologies, that tends to happen a lot.'

Colin gagged.

CHAPTER ELEVEN

Simply the Best

'Why are you walking outside in your dressing gown?'

Michael, the corpse, walked alongside Colin as they headed to the corner shop.

'What's wrong with what I'm wearing? People around here don't pay attention; they don't even notice you. And why does it bother you? At least I'm walking like a regular person, not spilling out my guts and dropping my eyes.'

Colin and Michael stepped into the shop.

'Well, they don't seem offer many choices here,' said Michael.

'You know, I've never been in a corner shop before; we usually order online.'

'Well, this isn't Waitrose or some fancy upscale market; it's just a corner shop where you can pick up necessities like bread or milk, things that you need on a day-to-day basis. And if you need more choice, then you need to drive or take the bus to Tesco or somewhere like that. And, of course, rich people like you can order online from Waitrose.'

'So, what's on your agenda today?' said

Michael.

'I'm sure you can start crafting the perfect eulogy for me if only I could recall half of my life. It's funny; maybe I have brain damage and it's made me forget almost my entire life.'

Colin glanced at Michael, still looking like a corpse. 'You don't say!'

They waited in the queue at the checkout where Ali was dealing with the customers.

'Hello there, my good friend Colin. I haven't properly thanked you for the last night. You turned into an instant hero by saving my life. It also spared you from footing our bills. That's what you call lucky, eh?'

'No, Ali, it's called an unexpected tragedy. You could have been my client today if I hadn't saved you.'

'I saved him?' chimed in Michael. 'I mean we did, we saved you.'

'What do you mean, we? Shut up you.'

Ali looked confused. Why are you telling me to shut up?'

'I meant to say, God and I, or your Allah, saved you. See you later, Ali.'

'Hey, hold on, Colin! Did you happen to see my wallet anywhere? I think I lost it somewhere, maybe in the cab. The driver charged me way too much.'

'Nope, I haven't seen your wallet. Maybe you dropped it in the taxi.'

Colin and Michael left the shop.

'It's good you have friends to chat with,' said Michael. 'I want to learn more about my life.'

'Great! Let's get started. Later today I'm going to visit someone who can tell me a bit more about your life. You can come with me, and see if you recognise him. But please stay quiet, and don't distract me when I'm speaking with him, okay?'

'Yup, I'll keep mum, I promise.'

Later that day Colin pressed the doorbell of a terraced house in a posh part of town. The front door swung open and a man wearing pyjamas pressed three black bin bags full of clothes into Colin's arms.

'Your late! I thought you were coming at 9 this morning to pick up these clothes. I'm wanting to go out, and I don't want to be messed about waiting for you. Anyway, there's a bunch of valuable clothing and shoes in there. Make sure they go to the charity shop. I'll check on them later,' he grumbled.

'Excuse me, I'm not here for a charity pickup,' I'm looking for this address, 144 Maple Avenue.

'Why didn't you say that earlier? I've been going on and on. So, who is it you are looking for?' And could you give me back my plastic bags? That's for charity, thank you.'

'Oh, sorry about that.'

Colin returned the bags.

'I'm searching for Stephen Bright.'

'Well, you're at the right address, and what do you want with Stephen Bright?'

'Fiona Jones gave me this address and said this person could provide more information about her son.'

The man's demeanour softened.

'You mean Fiona told you to do that?'

'Yeah, she did. And I assume you're Stephen, right?'

'Yes, that's me. Come in.'

Stephen led the way into the house.

'Please, have a seat. I apologize, I didn't catch your name.'

'I'm Colin Bott, the Celebrant. Here's my card as some form of identification.'

'So, you're going to be conducting Mikey's funeral?'

'Yes, that's correct, and I'm sorry for your loss. I believe you were a good friend of Michael and I'm trying to gather information about his life. I visited his parents yesterday, but they didn't provide much about their son. Mrs. Jones gave me your address, thinking you might be able to contribute something. The funeral's next Friday, so time is a bit tight.'

'I understand. I was devastated when I heard about Mikey. It feels like my world has been turned upside down. Oh, I apologize, where are my manners? Would you like a cup of tea or something, Colin?'

'Just a glass of water would be fine, thank you.'

Stephen headed to the kitchen, and Colin couldn't help but glance around the room. Thoughts swirled in his mind.

'So, dead Michael was right,' he thought. 'This guy's filthy rich. This Victorian flat probably has 2-3 bedrooms, not bad at all.'

Colin wandered around the room, eyeing the paintings and an expensive wall clock. Suddenly, his attention was drawn to a sculpture. Intrigued, he leaned in, using his reading glasses to examine it more closely.

'Holy shit, what the hell is that?'

The sculpture, made of a clay material was in the shape of a penis, and the head of it morphing into the face of Michael.

'Boo! It's me, I'm here and that's my face on there you know.'

Colin was startled, and jumped away at the sudden scare as Michael attempted to spook him.

Stephen appeared at the door, holding a tray of tea and biscuits.

'Are you okay Colin? I often get that same reaction when people see that remarkable sculpture. I hope you're impressed; I made it myself.'

'That thing?'

Colin replied, still recovering from the surprise.

'Yes, that thing. It was a gift, a symbol of our five years together. Mikey and I, as you may have gathered, were a couple. I'm sure Fiona must have mentioned that, didn't she?'

'No, she didn't Stephen. I didn't know about your relationship with Michael.'

Stephen's smile faded.

'Oh, I thought they or even Fiona might have mentioned us, Mikey and me.'

'I'm sorry about that Stephen.'

'It's okay. I just thought that Mikey's parents might have come to terms with it, now that their son is gone.'

Stephen was trying to hold back his emotions as he walked over to the window and stared out.

Michael whispered, 'I'm not gone yet, I'm still here.'

'I told you to stop popping up; you scared me! I nearly wet my pants. Stay quiet and let me do my job,' Colin whispered.

'And I don't know why you're whispering; he can't hear you,' said Mikey.

'So, as you see, he's my partner. It's not exactly what I was hoping for, or any magical feeling, but hey, it is what it is. Maybe we were in love. I can see his pain now,' Michael reflected.

Stephen turned away from the window, wiped his tears, and attempted to clear his throat.

'Anyway, Colin, I'd be happy to help you. Just ask me anything. I'm trying to recall the dates and places we've been, but I'm still coping with the situation right now.'

'I understand, Stephen. Just tell me what you remember about Michael when you were together.' Colin encouraged.

Stephen began to speak, recounting the beginning of his relationship with Michael.

'Mikey and I met at a club where I worked as a bartender. We started seeing each other, and I invited him to my sculpture class, where I teach clay sculpting. That's when I gave him that silly penis sculpture. Not one of my best creations. Mind you, I've made a lot of things like, a man's backside, or two men together in the act of lovemaking, would you like to see them?'

'No, thank you Stephen; I'm probably not artistic enough to appreciate them. Let's just focus on Michael's life for now.'

'Sure, as you wish. Anyway, that's how our beautiful relationship began. We travelled a lot, visited many countries. We were together for five years. The most memorable, yet regretful day was when we celebrated Mikey's 30th birthday. I wanted to surprise him. All our friends and even his parents were invited. I thought it would be a delightful surprise.'

'After that day, everything changed. The party was set up at the pub; everyone was in costume, the stage was prepared, and the food was decorated. Mikey was ecstatic that night, laughing, drinking, and even dressed in a Cher costume. I wore a Tina Turner outfit. I asked him to join me on stage to sing his favourite song, 'Simply the Best' by Tina Turner.'

Stephen started to sing the song, and Colin noticed the tears in his eyes.

'We sang "Simply the Best" together on stage. It was a fantastic night. And then we kissed, and I noticed his parents standing in a corner. Their eyes were full of hatred, especially his father. I didn't tell Mikey they were coming, I wanted it to be a surprise. And it was much more than a surprise for them. That's when I realised that he had never told them about this part of his life. He had never told them about me and our love for each other.'

Stephen began to cry again.

'After that, Mikey cut off ties with his parents. It was a complete shock for them to discover their son was gay. A highly educated surgeon, from a prominent family, how could this be. Everything changed. I'm not sure if it was good for me or Mikey, but it's always been him and me.'

Colin stopped writing; he felt sympathy for Stephen.

'I think I've gathered enough information about Michael, or Mikey, as you called him. I promise I'll do my best to honour him and his family.'

'Thank you for that, Colin, but I'm afraid I won't be able to hear it.'

'Why not? Don't you plan to attend the funeral?'

'It's not that. I wanted to bid farewell to Mikey, but I know his parents wouldn't be pleased to see me. I'm sure they also believe it's because of me that their son is no longer alive.'

'Don't dwell on that; We don't know what they're thinking. However, his mother gave me your address, so she must have considered you a significant part of Michael's life. Otherwise, she wouldn't have bothered sending me to you, right?'

'Fair point, Colin. That uplifts my spirits a bit, if you know what I mean.'

'So, that settles it. I won't pressure you to attend the funeral. But, as you said, it's the last chance to say goodbye.'

Colin stood up, leaving Stephen lost in thought. Unaware that Mikey was sitting beside him, absorbing Stephen's sorrow and pain, he walked away, leaving the two of them alone.

As the funeral day approached, Colin struggled to pull together the information for Michael Jones' eulogy. He was working on his lap top, when the screen started flickering intermittently.

'What's happening? Don't die on me now. I can't afford a new computer at the moment.'

Colin muttered in frustration.

'Ah ha, struggling financially, are we, Colin? Your lap top looks like it's from another era, Vintage, I'd say.' teased Michael.

'Please stop interrupting while I'm working. And don't mock my setup. It might be old, but it still works. I'm not tech-savvy, unlike some people. If I made more money, sure, I'd upgrade it,' Colin retorted.

'Well, you'll need more clients, and maybe a hundred corpses, to afford a new laptop.' quipped Michael.

'Yeah, right.'

Colin glared at Michael.

As Colin continued his work, Michael wandered around the flat, finally deciding to sit at the end of the bed.

'Don't even try.' warned Colin.

'What, sleeping in your bed? No chance. It looks like your duvet hasn't seen a wash in weeks, maybe months, or even a year.'

'Well, I don't fancy your dead body all over my bed, thank you very much. So, I'm done; are you ready to hear about your life, your eulogy?'

'Don't read it aloud. Just let me read it myself.'

'Alright, as my client, I'll give you your space. I'll be back; hunger calls. I'll check if Marco's got some fish or pie left. And stay away from my bed, I'm serious.'

Marco spoke as Colin entered the fish n chip shop.

'Hey Colin, I haven't seen you around lately. What you been up to?' Here's some extra chips, Mrs. Caine. Enjoy your meal,' Marco smiled at the customer.

'Seems like you're busy today, Marco, and your helper in the kitchen looks a bit frantic. He caught a glimpse of Mia scurrying around; she gave Colin a quick wave.

'Yeah, lots of takeout orders today, people love to relax and splurge at the end of the month when they get paid, which works out well for us.'

'Exactly, and the home delivery guys keep pouring in I expect,' said Colin.'

'And as for you, buddy, how's the ghost crowd treating you? Got a line of dead folks requesting your service?'

'Haha, I wish! Being a celebrant's not a walk in the park you know. I'm not sure how well it'll go. I might end up in a loony bin with the pressure.'

'Ah, your Sixth Sense scenario! Talking to the dead. So, it looks like you're either joining them, or checking into the madhouse,' Marco chuckled, leaving Colin with his thoughts.

Colin spotted Michael the corpse outside the shop, waiting for him.

'Hey, Marco, could you whip up my usual dinner? I'll be back in a bit. Hopefully, you won't be swamped by then.'

'You doing alright Michael?'

Michael walked, looking a bit down, and Colin trailed after him.

'Did you not like what I've written? Maybe it needs a bit more pizzazz or adventure, but I can only jot down what your parents and Stephen shared. Don't be so glum about it.'

'It's not that. It's just that something feels missing in my story, a gap that I wish I could remember.'

'I wish I could help, but your funeral is in two days. Maybe after that, things will clear up, and you can move on.'

'Colin, you don't get it. What's my purpose here with you? If it's about telling my story, then fine. Just read the whole eulogy you've prepared at the service. But I sense something's missing.'

They strolled along the streets; Colin noticed the curious glances from passers-by as he appeared to be chatting to an unseen person.

'Colin, how did I kick the bucket?'

'What? You're asking me? How the hell would I know?'

'I need to fill that gap in my life. How did I die? Why are most of my memories hazy? Sometimes I recall things, other times, it's a blur. You need to find out how and why I died. Did I off myself? Despite my estrangement from my parents, I seemed content with Stephen.'

'Maybe it all started with your last moments alive. You were at the train station. I remember seeing you that night Mia and I were waiting for the train. The news was murky about your death —uncertain if it was suicide or murder, but the newspapers said you ended up on the rails. Perhaps it had something to do with your work.

'You're a surgeon, right? Maybe some medical malpractice. Perhaps you cut off the wrong bit or left some of your tools inside someone. If so, you'll be here with me for a while. Not what I wanted, but tomorrow night, we'll hit the railway station for some answers. First, let me grab some dinner.'

Michael vanished into thin air, carried away by the wind.

'Hey, where are you off to? I promise I'll help you.'

Next day, it was the same morning routine for Colin—coffee, cereal, and toast. He strolled to his bedroom, peering out the window, and began chatting with his plants.

'Good morning, plants. Any blooms today? Lucifer not giving enough plant pee nourishment? They say lilies are tough to kill. Easy and hard, like a paradox, huh?'

He hadn't noticed Mia standing in the same spot where Mrs. Chan usually shot him dirty looks every morning—an unwelcoming start to his day. But today, it was different. All he could see was a beautiful Italian woman with long, sleek black hair and a stunning figure. Colin began to view her as an angel, and enjoyed sipping his coffee while Mia added the extra sugar. That is until Mia began her morning routine, brushing her teeth at the kitchen sink, gargling loudly, then smelling her underarms—not a good look.

'Yuck!'

Colin grimaced.

'Luci, where are you? Breakfast time!'

Colin meticulously prepared the eulogy, ensuring everything was just right. He even phoned the funeral director to confirm the arrangements for Michael's service. But as the day wore on, his client, the corpse, was a no-show. Colin grew anxious, wondering if he had upset him somehow. He had promised to accompany Michael to the station to uncover more about his death.

THE CELEBRANT

'Hello, Michael, are you here? Come on, man, we're heading to the station as promised. I'll help you out.'

Colin called out, but he was only met with silence.

'Michael, let's go. Are you okay? Don't tell me you've got cold feet for your own funeral, just like someone who'd run away before their wedding. Well, I know you already have cold feet; you passed away a week ago, ha-ha. Hey, that's a joke. Come on, let's tackle this together.'

But there was still no sign of Michael. Colin waited until midnight, eventually dozing off in front of his lap top.

'Luci where are you c'mon breakfast time.
Are you around Michael?'

Colin called out, scanning the room for any sign of him.

'Where the heck is he? For heaven's sake, I knew something bad was going to happen. I'm not dealing with a corpse ever again.'

Sipping his coffee, he paced around, engaged in an intense inner dialogue, pondering the impending events and what Michael might be up to.

'I know what I'll do,' he exclaimed suddenly.

Colin dashed out, and headed straight for

Marco's flat, knocking repeatedly on the door.

'Marco, open up! It's an emergency. Your shop is on fire!'

The door swung open abruptly.

'What fire?'

Marco looked puzzled.

'There's no fire! I've been knocking for 15 minutes. Why didn't you answer.'

Colin walked into the flat and noticed Marco's perspiration. He handed him a glass of water.

'What have you been up to this early morning? What stopped you hearing the loud banging at your door?'

Colin raised an eyebrow.

Marco just grinned in response.

'Never mind, don't answer. You're disgusting - really, at this hour?'

'Well, you do what you gotta do. I've been partnerless for years, so I have to find my own sources of enjoyment, you know?'

'Okay, okay, spare me the details. I just want to find out if you know any gypsy, or fortune teller, or a witch doctor, someone like that?'

'I'm not quite sure what you're asking for, mate.'

'I mean someone who can communicate with

the dead.'

'Oh, you mean like a ghostbuster?'

'No, more like the movie Ghost, you know, like Whoopi Goldberg's character.'

'Ah, you mean a medium.'

'Yeah, a spiritualist or something like that.'

'Hey Colin, have you heard of the 'Oracle of the Dead' in ancient Greece? It was a temple on a sacred hill where the living could meet the departed. They had mediums who communicated with those who hadn't crossed over, you know, to the light.'

Colin gave Marco a quizzical look.

'How do you know all this, Marco?'

'Well, I once got involved with a Medium who scared the life out of me. I nearly married her when I first arrived in the UK; I was naive and vulnerable. She lived in a caravan, one of those gypsies who talk to spirits or ghosts or something.'

'That's why we broke up, or at least that's what I thought. The real reason was the haunted caravan. Her husband died a few weeks before me, and I felt like his ghost was always around, watching us constantly, even during intimate times. Sometimes it felt like I was kissing her and, at the same time, someone else was... you know. It was terrifying, like we were in a threesome. If I hadn't fallen for Lola, I wouldn't have stayed there for more than a week.'

'So, Lola was her name? Was she a showgirl

with yellow feathers in her hair and a dress cut down to there?'

Colin started dancing like Barry Manilow.

'Shut up Colin, don't be ridiculous. Lola was her dog. She also loved watching us. I tried to take Lola with me when I left, but she caught us. I was trying to set Lola free from her cage one night. Poor Lola.'

'What are you talking about, Marco? Who's the person I'm going to talk to?'

'Oh, that woman. Her name's Carmen. Hold on, I think I still have her business card somewhere. She lived at the end of Forest Brae Road? It's so secluded there; I never understood how anyone could live in that area.'

Colin immediately headed out the door

'Hey, Colin, do me a favour. When you see her, tell her that I miss her a lot, and someday, I'll be with her.'

'You want me to say that to Carmen?'

'No, to Lola. And don't you ever mention my name to her.'

'To Lola?'

'No, to Carmen.'

Colin followed Forest Brae Road until he arrived at a caravan site. There were numerous caravans clustered together like a small village. It was a grimy and unsightly area. He asked a couple of men walking past, which was Carmen's caravan.

They directed him to the end of the site where a caravan stood out on its own. There was a pug in a cage outside the caravan looking very lonely, and whimpering as Colin walked towards it.

'You must be Lola. Marco misses you.'

Colin noticed the large thick chain around Lola's neck. She was not a happy dog, but she seemed to recognize Marco's name, and wagged her tail slightly.

'Give me 500 quid and you can have my dog,' a voice came from behind.

'Huh, I'm not here to buy a dog. I already have Lucifer at home, and I don't think he'd appreciate a new addition.'

'Wait, you can talk to Lucifer?'

'Oh, not that Lucifer, the devil or Satan or anything like that.'

'Let me guess, you're here because you want to connect with spirits, am I right?'

'Well, fairly obvious why I'm here, or maybe not. The sign there on the side of your caravan says – Carmen the Spiritualist, Medium, Fortune Teller, Plumber, Carpenter, Electrician. Looks like you're a Jack of all trades, huh? Or should I say Jill of all trades, and I'm not looking for a plumber.'

'Well, we've all got to make a living these days. It's a small community here, and nobody can afford to call a proper plumber or an electrician. They know I can communicate with the departed

—dead people like plumbers, construction workers, even doctors and ask for guidance and advice. They believe I can work wonders.'

'So, what if you can't fix things?'

'Well, I just tell them that the spirit expert is no longer residing within me.'

Carmen invited Colin inside the caravan.

'Sorry about the mess; I haven't had time to tidy up my mansion. Too busy working around the community. Just grab a seat, and I'll prepare tea. Would you like one?'

'No thank you, I'm good.'

Colin glanced around, feeling a bit spooked. Marco was onto something—this place was a chaotic mess, and it seemed haunted. There were skull heads of deceased animals hanging about, Halloween decorations that lingered all year. Numerous jars were filled with the preserved remains of rabbits, snakes, lizards, and various other creatures. But what drew his attention the most was a large black object, a penis, suspended in a sizable clear jar.

'Damn, Marco, you dodged a bullet getting out of here.'

Carmen arrived with a cup of tea.

'What was that you said?'

'Oh, nothing. Is that from a black...?'

'Yep, it is. But not what you're thinking; it's from a black horse, and yes indeed, it is a penis,' reassured Carmen.

'Ah, right.'

Colin sighed in relief.

'Shall we begin now and get down to business? Sorry, I didn't catch your name.'

'Well, you're a fortune teller; come on, take your best shot. What name do you think suits me?' Colin teased.

'Arsehole - that fits you.' Carmen shot back bluntly.

'That's not very nice.'

'Well, we're not here to play guessing games. I have a lot on my plate. Shall we begin?'

'I'm a celebrant, Colin Bott by name. Perhaps you could add that to your list of job skills; it might be handy for a small community like this. Conducting a funeral service and...'

Carmen wore an expression of irritation, giving Colin a poker face.

'Alright, alright. I'm here to find out where my friend is. He's been missing since yesterday. I haven't felt his presence, even though he passed away a couple of weeks ago. That's why I'm here. Otherwise, I'd be at the police station inquiring about a missing person.'

Carmen remained unmoved, observing Colin without doing anything.

'Yeah, as I was saying... Are you alright? Aren't you going to bring out your crystal ball or cards or something?'

'Nope, those are old tricks. I don't do that anymore. Just go on, tell me more.'

'I heard you can communicate with the deceased. I need to learn about this person's life. The funeral's tomorrow. If you could help me connect with him, maybe ask him to reach out to me? We've spoken before. Let him know that I'm a good listener and I promise to help him understand his death, wherever he is right now, ask him to come back.'

'So, how much are we talking about here? What package do you want?'

'Eh? What do you mean by, package?'

'Listen, if you want to talk to a dead pet, it's 20 quid. 30 for the younger generation, and 50 pounds for the oldies.'

'Can you talk to animals also?'

'Yes, it's the cheapest, but probably harder to understand. And it depends. I only do four-legged pets: cats, dogs, rabbits, hamsters, that sort.'

'Why not the same price? They're all dead anyway,' Colin pointed out.

'Alright, let me break it down for you. The cheapest are the animals; their owners accept whatever they say. Younger ones, from children to teens, can be a bit challenging. They argue, are more aggressive, and think they know everything. Now, the older ones, 70 to 100, take a lot of effort. Many suffer from ailments like dementia, making it tough.'

'Got it. What about someone around 30? They're not as hard to handle as teens or the elderly. Could I get a discount, say, 25 quid?'

'Listen, this isn't a walk in the park for me. The 30-year-old is not part of my standard price list. It's 40 quid, take it or leave it.'

Colin didn't argue.

'Give me your hand, hold tight,' she said,

Colin was thinking he was finally getting a real, genuine medium.

'So, this person you want to talk to. Have you seen or touched him? Any communication in your dreams?'

'It's a man, 30 years old. No, he hasn't talked to me in dreams. He talks to me when I'm awake; he was around for a while and suddenly disappeared without any reason.'

'Okay, so ghosts or spirits have three different stages. The third stage is when they can wander about, visit loved ones, and cause some spooky activities. But when it's time for them to transition, they become apparitions. These folks are in a waiting zone, not quite dead but waiting for whatever comes next.'

'Like being in a coma?' Colin suggested.

'Similar idea.' Carmen agreed.

'In the second stage, they're the nasty ones. Best to stay away. They're in denial, dead but resisting acceptance. They are powerful due to their prolonged stay among the living. They've learned to harness energy, move things, touch, even possess bodies. Ever seen 'The Exorcist?'

'What the hell?' Colin reacted with fear.

'Yeah, scary, right? But I'm not saying your ghost is like that. Possession by a devil is different. I mean, is your ghost one of the nasty ones? Because that's an extra 50 quid.'

'I'm pretty sure he's just dead, and I feel sorry for him,' Colin replied.

Carmen looked confused.

'What I mean is, according to his mother's description, he seems like a nice person. So, what's the first stage?'

'In the first stage, you're on the waiting list, sitting right beside the door, waiting to be called. When the door opens, you have to walk toward the light; it's time to cross over. But I can't knock on that door. No one opens it unless you're ready to go through, and there's no turning back. I don't want to be in that stage, not yet.'

'I hope he's in the first stage, just waiting to be called and cross over,' Colin said optimistically.

'Okay, let's begin. I'll start a sentence, and you'll continue it, no questions asked. I can't do it alone, so are you with me?'

Carmen was waiting for answer from Colin.

'Yeah, I'm with you, Carmen. Let's call him.'
'Alright, what's his name again?'

'It's Michael, or Mikey for short. Let's call him Mikey.'

'Okay, Mikey, Mikey, are you here? We're here to ask your permission to talk with us.'

After a moment of silence, nothing happened.

'Mikey, Mr. Bott wants to talk to you. He wants some information regarding...'

'Hey, it's me. Can we talk? Mikey, it's Colin. I'm still here waiting for you. I promised to help you in any way I can. Give me a sign or visit where I live. Your service is tomorrow. I really want you to move on, to cross over the rainbow.'

They continued holding hands, eyes closed.

'Can you feel him, Carmen?'
'Oh yeah, I can feel his presence all over this room. He wants to speak to you.'
'Mikey is communicating with you now, Colin.'

He scanned the room, but there's no sign of Michael's presence.

'Mikey is communicating with you, Colin.'
'Alright, so what's Mikey like?'

Keeping his eyes open, he gazed intensely at Carmen, eager to hear her description.

'Mikey was around 30, had caring parents, he passed away a few weeks back. He was quite handsome, muscular, the kind of guy women would be attracted to. Rough appearance, very manly, tall—seemed like a plumber or construction worker.'

As Carmen spoke, Colin noticed a framed picture behind her that matched her description of Mikey.

'Okay, enough of this nonsense. I should have known better. I'd better leave now.'

'Mikey! Wait, please don't go. Mr. Bott wants to talk to you more! Mikey, wait!" Carmen pleaded, then opened her eyes.

'I'm sorry, Mr. Bott, they only communicate once. I can't call him again unless you pay.'

'Oh really? Who's that in the picture behind you?'

'That's my deceased husband. Do you know him?'

'Well, I'm quite certain who you're talking to right now—your deceased husband. This is a waste of time.'

'I could try again, for half the price if you want.'

'No, thank you. I'm leaving. He quickly left the caravan, and outside, he saw Lola, her eyes pleading for rescue.

'Don't look at me like that. Oh, what the heck.' He grabbed the dog from the cage.

'Run, Colin run.'

CHAPTER TWELVE

Goodbye Mikey it's time

It's as bustling as ever at the train station—everyone moving so quickly, some even running. It's hard to stop anyone; it's like they're all in a perpetual rush and no time to talk. That's the reputation of city dwellers—aloof or unapproachable. But things have changed a bit. While people are still unwilling to engage in conversation, there are lots of staff at the station you can ask for directions or help.

Mikey sat on one of the benches, surveying his surroundings. Vague memories of the accident night started to emerge. He watched the crowded platform, the urgency in the air. He stood up and moved towards the approaching train. The lights and sounds swirled around him. Suddenly, a memory struck—a phone call with his dad.

'I'm not asking for much, Dad. I just wanted to let you know I'm planning to propose to Stephen, start a family. I'm not asking for your permission; I'm informing you before I ask Stephen. It's your call if you want to be involved or even attend our wedding.'

'You're asking the wrong person, Michael. I don't want to be part of your circus. You're old enough to make your own choices. You've chosen this path. I once had a son who was respected. That's how I want to remember him.'

He abruptly ended the call.

'Dad! Please!' But he was gone.

Putting his phone away Mikey stumbled and fell onto the tracks just as the train approached. It was too late for anyone to intervene. The onlookers were stunned by the horrific accident.

Michael was taken aback by the stark reality of his demise. He stood still as people passed by his ghostly form. That one conversation with his dad seemed to mark the end of everything for him. Departing without bidding farewell to the only person who failed to embrace him for who he truly was. Moreover, Stephen was unaware of Michael's imminent proposal for a lifelong commitment.

Fiona Jones knocked on her husband's home office door, holding a cup of coffee.

'The door's open,' came the voice from within.

'Here's your coffee. I noticed you hadn't had your usual afternoon tea.'

'Thank you.' said Robert without raising his head to acknowledge Fiona. She slowly backed away, wanting to say more.

Robert raised his head.

'If you're wondering if I've done anything about tomorrow's funeral arrangements for your son, everything is in order. I've spoken to the funeral director. I didn't bother inviting anyone, not that I wanted to. I doubt anyone would bother showing up.'

'What makes you think they won't attend our son's funeral? I've invited some friends and relatives for tomorrow. They inquired about an afternoon tea gathering, and they understand it's meant to be a quiet service. Everything's sorted.'

'Good. Then there's nothing more to discuss. And I won't be going to your son's funeral,' said Robert

Fiona stood her ground before him.

'I have only one husband whom I respect, love, and have obeyed since we married. I gave him a son—the son he always desired. Intelligent, obedient, respectful. He excelled in his studies and all activities just to make you proud. Once, when he was ten, I asked him what made him happy. His reply – "I'm happy when Daddy is proud of me." He was always a good son. For the last time, maybe you can bid him farewell. I'm not asking you to forgive him because he did nothing to warrant forgiveness. It's me who should ask for your forgiveness, because I've always known who my son truly was.'

Her husband kept his head down, engrossed in his writing.

'Be a father to your son, just this once in your life. Parents shouldn't punish their children simply because they didn't comply with their desires. It's not an excuse to claim, it's for their best or that we know what's right for them. Our children aren't possessions; we're here to guide and protect them, just as our parents did before us. If I can't change your mind, for God's sake, I'll be burying two people tomorrow.'

With those words, she walked away.

At 2 am, just a few hours before the funeral, Colin jolted awake, clearly uncomfortable.

'For heaven's sake! Don't startle me like that again.'

Michael sat by the bed, watching Colin.

'I didn't mean to disturb you. You sleep like a baby.'
'Maybe that's what you think. Ever since these corpses started talking to me, I've been plagued by nightmares, and not just in my dreams. Where have you been? I searched for you, even went to the station yesterday to see if you were there.'

'I did go to there to try and figure out what happened to me. It wasn't a pleasant memory; it was a horrific scene for those who witnessed my death. At least now I have some closure.'

Colin was sitting up in bed, half-naked, draped in a partial blanket; Michael sat at the edge of the bed, eyeing his partially exposed body.

'What's your answer, then? And why the interest in my body?'.

'I was just observing your nipples. Do you have three? That's bizarre.'

'Don't be stupid; that's not a third nipple; it's a mole. Anyway, about your answer, I hope it helped you find peace and able to move on.'

'Don't worry; my sentiments are mutual. I don't fancy sticking around with you forever. But if you could do me a favour, I might finally rest in peace. Can you?' Michael inquired.

'Absolutely. I'll do whatever it takes to assist you, as long as we part ways afterward. Not that I don't enjoy your company, but I won't miss our arguments and the banter.'

'As I said, Colin, my feelings are mutual. I hope you won't miss me,' said Michael.

'Oh, I'm quite sure I won't.'

Late that day Colin sat in his car in the crematorium car park.

He was frantically shuffling through his papers and reading the eulogy page by page. Suddenly there was a loud knock on his car window. It was Kevin.

'Hey, we're about to start. Everyone's looking for you.'

Colin stepped out of the car.

'Are there a lot of people inside?'

'Maybe about a couple of hundred, and the

hearse hasn't arrived yet. So, you're lucky.'

Colin felt a surge of panic.

'What?'

'Just kidding! But you're a bit late. There's only about twenty people, and most won't even notice. And at least your sober. We had someone yesterday taking a service, and he was so drunk he could hardly speak. He managed to get through the eulogy without falling over, but when they played the reflection music, he sat down, fell asleep and started snoring. It was hilarious.'

'What kind of celebrant was that?' Colin asked.

'A priest,' Kevin chuckled.

'You're not helping, Kevin. I'm not late; I'm dead-on time and I'm just a bit nervous. Maybe after ten services, I'll get the hang of it.'

'More like eighty to a hundred services before you'll get the hang of it.' Kevin teased.

Colin shot him a serious look.

'I hope you're kidding. Anyway, let's go. The hearse is on its way.'

The people in the crematorium stood as the coffin was carried in. The music playing was, "Simply the best by Tina Turner". There were six people carrying the coffin followed by the funeral director.

Colin, had joined the procession, and as he

moved forward, he felt at ease and looking around at the attendees in the crematorium. Although he was proud of the dignity he exuded, he had a strong desire to sway with the music; it was a fitting tribute to Michael.

Among the attendees were individuals in black suits and ties, projecting an air of formality. They were probably Michael's doctor colleagues.

However, Colin couldn't help grinning when he saw some of Michaels personal friends. There were drag queens in vibrant, glittering clothing, dancing along to Tina Turner's music. Colin remembered some of his time spent with Michael, reminding him of their camaraderie. Colin felt transported to a dreamlike state, when he caught sight of Michael, not as the corpse he once knew, but as a refined gentleman in a pristine white suit. He was smiling warmly from the corner of the crematorium stage.

Colin spotted Kevin seated in one of the aisle seats and he signalled to Colin to control his smile.

Unfortunately, Stephen was nowhere to be seen.

Colin began speaking, delivering the Eulogy while adding some alterations to Michael's story. His changes led to laughter among the people there which pleased Colin. They especially enjoyed Stephen's funny anecdotes about their shared experiences.

Seeing Mrs. Jones' laughter during the

describing of her son's stories, Colin realized that Michael hadn't been alone during the years they lost contact. It was apparent that Michael had a happy life, even until his final moments.

The unexpected presence of Mr. Robert Jones took Colin by surprise; it wasn't part of the arrangement. As the reflective music ended, Colin noticed Mr. Jones approaching with a piece of paper in hand. Instantly, Colin understood what was needed.

'Ladies, gentlemen, Michael's father, Mr. Robert Jones, will share a few words.'

Fiona Jones was caught off guard, tears welling in her eyes as she watched her husband walk down the aisle.

The room fell silent as everyone awaited what Mr. Jones had to say.

'Most of you here probably know my son better than I do, which is quite ironic. Michael, he's my son, my only son. He always heeded my words, ensuring I was content with him. Every time he achieved something—awards, medals—I saw that look in his eyes, a look I could never quite comprehend. Was it happiness from his accomplishments, or was it solely to please me? He excelled in everything, making me proud to be his father. Yet, these achievements, they seem to reflect more on me. People commend me, saying, 'You must be proud of yourself; you did well, you're a good father.' But I don't deserve to be his father.

I'm selfish and unfeeling.'

Tears streamed down his face uncontrollably, expressing the inner agony and torment he felt, realizing the pain he inflicted on his son.

His wife was holding her breath, her smile reflecting her enjoyment and appreciation for every heartfelt word spoken by her son's father.

Robert continued.

'There's no use crying over spilled milk, as they say. I can't embrace you, Michael. I'll never again see your face or hear your voice. But I believe you can hear mine. I apologize for not supporting the life you wanted, for taking away your time with your mother, and for my wife's sake too. My son, you've given me the most incredible fatherhood experience one could ask for. And to Stephen, thank you for standing by my son, and I'm sorry for your loss.'

He stepped down and approached his wife; they shared a heartfelt embrace.

'Thank you, Dad.' Michael whispered, hearing and forgiving every word his father had spoken.

Colin proceeded to read the poem given by Stephen, penned by an unknown author. It was Michael's desire for this poem to express his love for his father during his funeral.

As We Look Back

As we look back over time
We find ourselves wondering .....
Did we remember to thank you enough
For all you have done for us?
For all the times you were by our sides
To help and support us .....
To celebrate our successes
To understand our problems
And accept our defeats?
Or for teaching us by your example,
The value of hard work, good judgment,
Courage and integrity?
We wonder if we ever thanked you
For the sacrifices you made.
To let us have the very best?
And for the simple things
Like laughter, smiles and times we shared?
If we have forgotten to show our
Gratitude enough for all the things you did,
We're thanking you now.
And we are hoping you knew all along,
How much you meant to us.

'Let us end by playing one of Dr. Michael Jones favourite songs, dedicated to his dad.'

Colin announced, casting a glance at Michael in the corner.

'Thank you, Colin.' were Michael's parting words as he gradually disappeared.

The music commenced, signalling the end of the ceremony.

Father and Sons by Cat Stevens

*It's not time to make a change
Just relax, take it easy
You're still young, that's your fault
There's so much you have to know
Find a girl, settle down
If you want you can marry
Look at me, I am old, but I'm happy* ....

In the reception area, a satisfied man observed the entire funeral service on the small monitor. Stephen wiped away his tears, sporting a smile on his face. As he walked away from the crematorium, he uttered,

'Until we meet again.'

Later that day Stephen was in his apartment when he heard a knock at his door.

When he opened it, a man handed him a brown envelope without a word, and immediately left.

Stephen was, a bit puzzled by the lack of an address or stamp on the envelope. He settled on the sofa, sipping his coffee. He was nearly done packing the large boxes, preparing to move out of the apartment. To his astonishment, the envelope contained a letter from Michael:

To my life partner and best friend. This is my wedding gift to you.

Hope it brings you joy.
Love you always, Mikey

In Stephen's hand was the deed to the apartment with his name on it. When he shook the envelope, an engagement ring fell out. Tears and laughter mingled.

'You cheeky bastard Mikey, you never fail to surprise me.'

CHAPTER THIRTEEN

You are my Sunshine

The Hospital was busy with new incoming patients; there had been a fire in the High Street. Everyone was busy and headed to the emergency room.

The mother looked visibly anxious and distraught as she paced back and forth in the hallway, her eyes darting towards the operating room every few seconds. She seemed to be on the verge of tears, and her hands trembled. Her entire body was tense, and she seemed unable to relax, even for a moment. Despite her attempts to remain composed, it was clear that she was struggling to keep her emotions in check, and the stress of the situation was taking a toll on her.

She saw the nurse emerging from the operating room, heading towards the nurse station. She spoke to a colleague about the urgent need for more medicine and supplies in the emergency room. The mother stopped the nurse and her worried questions poured out:

'How is she? Is she okay? How's my baby?'

'She's a fighter, she'll be okay. She's too young not to keep going,' said the nurse.

Upon hearing that her baby would survive and was fighting, the mother felt a rush of hope and relief.

Colin parked his car in front of the fish and chip shop and saw Marco cleaning the windows. Marco had refurbished his shop and had put up a new neon sign with different colors that could be seen from a distance. The sign was so bright that any passing motorist could possibly be blinded and cause an accident.

'Marco, the shop looks amazing! I love the new neon sign; they'll be able to see your shop from space!'

'Thank you, Colin! I'm glad you like it. It was a lot of work, but I think it was worth it.'

'Definitely. It's hard to miss your shop now with those bright colors and lights.'

'That was the idea! I wanted to make sure everyone knew we were here, and that we're open for business.'

'Well, you definitely achieved that. And the new paint job looks great too. I can see why. You've put a lot of effort into making your shop stand out. I'm sure it'll attract even more customers.'

'That's the plan! I want to keep improving and growing my business. And with feedback from customers like you, I know I'm on the right track.'

'Absolutely.' Colin agreed.

As Colin admired Marco's refurbished shop, he noticed the new menu, new cash register, and display cabinet inside the shop. He was curious about how Marco was able to afford all of the expenses for the refurbishment.

'So, how did you manage to make your shop look like it was on the Las Vegas strip? Did you rob a bank or something? How were you able to afford all of this?'

Marco chuckled nervously.

'Well, it took some serious saving and a loan from the bank, but it was worth it.'

Colin wasn't convinced and prodded further.

'Don't lie to me mate. It's none of my business, but I hope you didn't go to a loan shark or something? You know, like that sleazy Ali from the corner shop.'

Marco tried to avoid eye contact and muttered,

'Well, actually it *was* Ali who helped me out. He said I could just pay him back monthly.'

'What! Ali? The same Ali who tried to con me on that date with Mia. That Ali?'

Marco nodded sheepishly.
'Well, there's only one Ali around here, right?'

Colin couldn't help but laugh.

'Man, you really are in deep with Ali. You better watch your back; he might start demanding payment in the form of free fish n chips.!'

'Well, I need to compete with the fast-food

shop next door. Since they opened their business, less and less customer are coming to my shop anymore.'

Colin's became a bit more serious listening to Marco's tale of woe.

'Listen, I understand that competition can be tough, and I think your flashy new look will bring in more business. But it looks like you're trying to copy the other food outlets on the street with bright colours and neon lights. You're turning your shop into something it's not.'

Marco looked down, feeling a bit guilty.

'I know, Colin. I just didn't know what else to do. I was desperate to keep my business afloat.'

'I get it, but there are other ways to stand out from the competition without resorting to copying them. You're a talented businessman, Marco. You just need to think outside the box.'

Marco looked up, seeing a glimmer of hope.

'Do you really think so?'

'Absolutely,' Colin said with a sarcastic smile.

'Oh, Colin why are you making a joke all the time.'

'Marco, did you hear about the Italian chef who died? '

'No, what happened?'

'He pasta-way. That's a joke Marco.

Marco rolled his eyes.

'That was terrible Colin.'

'Come on, it was funny! Alright, alright. How about this one? Why did the tomato turn red?

'I don't know, why? Colin.'

'Because it saw the salad dressing!'

Marco laughed

'Okay, that one was a bit better.'

'Glad you liked it. But seriously, let's get back to business So, how much did you spend for all of this?'

'I don't know, Ali said not to worry about paying him back, but now I'm paying him £2,000 a month!'

'Two grand a month! Marco, that's enough to buy a small island in the Caribbean!

'I know, I know. I feel like I'm drowning in debt.'

'Well, I guess you could always sell your shop and move to that island you just bought. How long are you going to pay him?'

'For a year.'

'A year? That's crazy! You'll end up paying him £24,000 in total!'

'I know, I'm starting to regret this decision.'

'You really fucked up this time Marco.'

There was a minute of silence between the two of them.

'Don't worry, Marco. We'll find a solution,

perhaps we can always start a Go Fund Me page for you.'

'Ha! That's funny, Colin. I don't think anyone would give me money to pay Ali.'

'You never know, Marco. Stranger things have happened.'

'I guess you're right, Colin. Thanks for cheering me up. I needed that.'

'Don't worry, I'll keep an eye on Ali, and see if we can come up with a solution. I better go now; Lucifer is waiting for his can of tuna. He's been a good boy these past few days, always staying at home. And he hasn't been going to the care home anymore and annoying the old people.

Colin was about to leave the shop.

'Hey, I forgot to thank you for delivering the package to Stephen, I owe you one,' said Colin with a grin.

'Oh, it's no problem at all. But it did cost me 30 quid to get that envelope, so you owe me that.

'What? Why? Did you have to bribe someone or something?'

'No, I had to pay the janitor to open the locker in the gym just to get that envelope.'

'Did I not tell you to write down the combination number of the locker?' said Colin. He was trying to remember if he had given Marco specific instructions.

'Well, I lost the piece of paper, Colin. Sorry about that. But I managed to deliver the brown envelope okay. Inside was an engagement ring and the deed of the property; everything was there like you said.'

'Wait a minute, I didn't tell you what was inside the envelope. I just asked you to get the brown envelope and deliver it to the address that I gave you.'

'Relax, Colin. I just checked what was inside the package. I didn't want to deliver dead body parts, or something illegal, you know.'

This made Colin chuckle.

As Colin headed towards the door, Marco couldn't help but ask.'

'Hey, Colin, what's all this about jewelry items from dead people? Is there anything that you want to share?'

Colin waved his hand.

'The lesser you know, Marco, the better. See you later.'

While Colin was entering the door to his flat, two ambulances, one after another screeched past.

'Must be a big accident,' thought Colin.

The next day Colin was on his way to another job at the crematorium. This was the fifth one he has taken on in the last two months since becoming a celebrant. While the work helped him pay the rent and cover his expenses, he was uncertain whether it was worthwhile as the pay was not substantial enough.

Coli walked towards the carpark of the crematorium after the service. He felt content after talking to the family and receiving compliments about the service. He was proud of his work. It had been a long time since he had encountered a talking corpse without any chaos. He wondered if the medicine he had taken helped him avoid the hallucinations of seeing dead people.

As he walked towards his old car, he saw Kevin sitting on a bench in the cemetery holding his shovel. Colin walked toward Kevin and sat beside him.

'Hey, Kev taking a break, eh? You must be busy these past weeks, lots of people to bury.'

'Yeah, it's been a busy week, lots of dead people waiting to be buried.'

'Is everything ok with you Kev, you look stressed out.'

'Nah, just tired and bored maybe. I've been doing this job for many years now; I can even dig graves with my eyes closed.'

Colin wanted to lighten the mood.

'Well, at least you don't see dead corpses or any ghosts around here, everything is normal. Imagine if the dead people start to talk to you and started to annoy you. You would then rather be bored than talking to dead people. And if they started dancing to Thriller, then that would be a different story.'

Kevin looked at Colin and started to laugh.

'You're right, I'd rather be bored than having a zombie dance party in the graveyard.'

They both laughed.
'I think I should get a proper job Kev, this job is not giving me enough work, I'm not sure if it will speed up.'
'Whoa, Colin! You're sounding like a quitter. Remember when you said you were going to be the best darn celebrant the world has ever seen?'
'Yeah, I remember that, but I can't pay my bills with just 5 jobs. The competition is fierce out there'
'Well, you know what they say, Colin. If at first, you don't succeed, try, try again! And if that doesn't work, just become a professional couch potato. I hear they make a lot of money these days.'

Colin sighed.

'I've tried, Kev. Door-to-door funeral services are like trying to sell sunscreen to vampires. No interest.'

'Are you throwing in the towel then?' Kevin asked.

'Nah, not entirely. Just contemplating how to make celebrant competition vanish into thin air. Maybe I'll start a magician act'.

Kevin raised an eyebrow.

'So, you're saying you're not good enough for these folks?'

Colin shrugged.

'I think there are many Funeral Directors and arrangers who are really friendly with certain celebrants and give them all their work. It's the old pals act. Which I suppose is okay, but I also think there is some money changing hands. Do you know what I mean Kev. So, how can I compete with that? Maybe I just have to show them how professional I am. Because to be honest, some the celebrants I've met are pretty crap. Some of them don't even look smart.'

Kevin nodded.

'But seriously, mate, have some patience. Quality over quantity, remember?'

Colin sighed.

'Yeah, but in these dire times, my cat Lucifer might start to consider me as a delicacy if I don't get more celebrant gigs. He's got a refined taste in food!'

Kevin laughed.

'Look Colin, there's one of your competitors, he's the oldest celebrant around.'

An old man walked out of the crematorium.

He was shaking hands with everyone and there was a fancy car waiting for him. As he stepped into the car he waved to Colin. He waved back.

'Look at him go! Seems like he's always got work.'

Kevin nodded

'Everyone knows him. He's one of the pioneers, the first celebrant here. Probably going to retire soon. You should chat with him sometime, learn a thing or two.'

Colin whispered.

'Is that Peter McIntyre, the legendary Peter McIntyre?'

'Yup, one of the celebrants from the '90s, I think.'

'So, why's he waving at me? He doesn't know me; we've never met.' Colin wondered aloud.

'It's not you he's waving at, mate. It's the person behind you—the celebrant taking the next service.'

Colin turned to look and chuckled. It's the Irish leprechaun.

'Have you crossed paths with him before?' Kevin asked.

'Nah, caught a glimpse of him when I was doing all my research into being a celebrant. But let me tell you, the mourners at his services found him duller than dishwater.' Colin whispered, only to hear a voice behind them.

'Who's dull as dishwater?' Said the leprechaun. Colin spun around.

'Oh, hi there, I'm Colin Bott, and I'm a...'

'I know you! You're that new celebrant. Seen you around. But let's be real, are you here for the service or just checking me out, and looking to steal some of my stuff?'

'No way sir, I don't need to copy anyone's work, beside I don't think I need to.'

The Leprechaun gave a smile.

'We'll see each other again no doubt. Anyway, I have to go, I have a service to do. This is my sixth job today, not quite busy enough though. Nice to meet you, Colin Bott. By the way my name is Falker Menace.' He waved his hand as he walked away.

Colin grinned and waved back.

'Catch you later, Falker!'

Kevin, stifled a chuckle.

'You almost said something else there.'
Colin winked.

'Oh, did I? Must be the Irish accent playing tricks on me!'

Next morning Colin was waiting in the reception area of the outpatient department at the local hospital. Waiting for his name to be called. He had a bad cramp in the lower part of his stomach. He'd been to his local doctor and he arranged an immediate x-ray and a specialist to find out what was causing the cramp.

Colin sat in the waiting room, and picked up a newspaper. He noticed a distressed woman pacing in front of him, and whispering to herself. He deliberately avoided looking at her, he didn't want to engage in conversation, especially with someone in distress. He focused on reading the newspaper, covering his face.

After waiting almost an hour Colin walked up to the reception desk.

'Excuse me Miss, I have an appointment at 8. 30 this morning and it's almost 9 now. Can you tell me what's happening. I have an appointment at the dentists at ten o'clock.'

The not so interested receptionist continued to look at her computer.

'Name?'
'Ah, Colin Bot.'
'Age?'
'53'
'Doctor's name?'
'Dr. Patel'
'Address?'
'65 Nottingham Street.'
'I've got it, all your information is here.'

Colin was muttering to himself, 'why the hell did you not ask me these questions before?'

'Excuse me are you saying something?'

'Nope, I never said a word, but I've been sitting here for over half an hour now, and I know you like patients to be on time for their appointments.'

'Well, I'm afraid Dr. Patel is running late; he is in surgery at the moment. But he will be here if you want to wait; he will be here shortly.

Colin scratched his head.

'Late? I've been here for ages; I could've learned how to knit a sweater by now.'

The receptionist went back to looking at her computer, uninterested.

Colin went back to his seat but he could hear snippets of the receptionist's conversations when she picked up the phone. She was speaking to someone in the mortuary.

'Morty, that's out of my hands. The family seems to be opting for a more cost-effective service, not our usual funeral director. But no worries, another one will swing by this afternoon, so you won't be swamped at the morgue. Alright? Oh, and Morty, make sure to pass my friend's business card to the incoming funeral director. Got it? Bye.'

Colin muttered to himself in frustration.

'Yeah, that's it, the networking game! That's why I'm not getting enough gigs. It's all about who knows who.'

He stood up, trying to catch the receptionist's attention once more, inadvertently irritating her in the process.

'What?'

The receptionist finally finished her typing and looked up from her computer.

'Listen, I have a dentist appointment and I can't keep waiting here. Could you reschedule my appointment, please?'

Colin was hoping for a favour.

'I can't do that. Go back to your local GP and ask them to reschedule,' she replied brusquely.

'Thank you, Miss, you've been a real gem. Could you point me in the direction of the morgue?'

'Ground floor, turn right, past the laundry room, last room on the right.'

The receptionist paused, curious about his odd inquiry.

'Why do you need the morgue?'

Colin quickly backtracked.

'Oh, did I say morgue? My bad, I meant the toilet! Bye!'

He hurriedly walked away, leaving the

receptionist puzzled by his abrupt change of destination.

Colin strolled down the hospital hallway, in the basement. There was a fluorescent light not working properly. It was flickering and adding an eerie vibe.

'Hello ... anybody here?'

He looked around, his nerves kicking in as he continued through the quiet corridor, despising the hospital smell. Suddenly, he spotted a shadow darting from one room to another, sending him into a panic.

'Oh no, not another corpse asking for favours.'

He muttered nervously, feeling the tension rise.

Then, a simultaneous scream echoed through the hallway as a hand touched Colin's shoulder, followed by another cold hand on his own.

'Ahhh!' they both yelled in fright until Colin realized it must be Morty, the Mortuary attendant.

'You scared the living daylights out of me, man! I nearly lost it there,' said Morty.

'Sorry, mate. I thought you were one of those creepy corpses chasing me.' Colin chuckled.

'What? Do I look like a corpse?' Morty raised an eyebrow, glaring at Colin.

'No, no, no! That's not what I meant at all. It's just so dark in here, and with the lights going on and off, I didn't see you.'

'Because it's dark, eh? And cause I'm black, is that what you're saying?'

Morty was teasing, and giving Colin a mock serious look.

'Oh, no! I didn't mean... I mean, I didn't want to... you know...'

Colin stumbled, feeling embarrassed.

'Hahaha, I'm pulling your leg, mate! Come on in. Are you from the funeral directors here to pick up a body? Mila the receptionist said that you're from a funeral director, right?'

'Yup' Colin replied, telling a little fib.

'Great, can you lend a hand for a minute? I've got a tiny issue.'

Colin followed him, and as they went into the white tiled mortuary, his reaction was immediate.

'Holy shit!'

A rather large gentleman lay on the floor, completely naked and face down, displaying an impressively sizable backside.

'Yeah, that's what I said, a tiny issue. But that's a colossal behind—biggest one I've ever seen.'

Morty quipped, trying to lighten the

situation.

'Are we going to chop this guy up? It might take us a day or two to finish.'

'Morty glanced at Colin, visibly shocked.

'What did you say? Are you crazy?'

'I'm just messing around, mate. Relax, I'm not some serial killer.'

Colin reassured Morty, tapping his shoulder before walking around the body on the floor. He then noticed another body on the opposite side of the mortuary lying on an autopsy table. It was a woman, and he felt a surge of curiosity.

'Listen mate, if you're not here for a gore fest, I'd suggest steering clear. That one arrived after a nasty car accident. So, about that helping hand you promised...'

'What's the plan?' Colin asked, unsure about the situation.

'Well, you take the head, and I'll handle the feet. On the count of three, you lift, and we'll get him back on the table.' Morty directed.

'Why do I have to grab the head? You take that, I'll handle the feet.'

'No weight difference between legs and feet, mate. Feet, legs, and that great backside are heavier than the head. Come on, before the boss shows up! I can't afford to get sacked in my first week.'

Colin, feeling the pressure, wiped his brow.

'Alright, on three; one two three – lift.'

Together, they managed to reposition the body onto the stainless-steel table. Morty swiftly tidied up, and covered the lower half with a white sheet.

He grinned at Colin.

'What's with the smile?' said Colin

'Come on, mate, don't you recognize the man?'

Morty teased.
Colin remained puzzled.

'Not really, but he does seem familiar. I think I've come across him before.'

'Of course, you've seen him! He's all over TV, the face of countless commercial ads.'

Colin examined the corpse's face closely.

Simultaneously, they both burst into singing the commercial jingle.

'Go Compare!'

They erupted into laughter, sharing the unexpected moment.

'I was just trying to impress my girlfriend, you know. She hates this guy on TV, so I thought I'd snap a selfie. Next thing I know, oops, he's on the floor.'

'You're in for a lecture from your boss, for not

respecting the dead.' Colin warned.

'Yeah, I'm bracing myself. By the way, I'm Morty short for Montgomery. Haven't caught your name?' He extended his hand.

'I'm Colin Bott, at your service. Here, take my card.'

Morty glanced at the card.

'Wait, I thought you worked for the funeral directors, here to collect the body.'

'Nope, just sneaking in some brochures and cards for potential gigs with the funeral director.'

Colin confessed with a grin.

'You're joking, right?' Morty looked bewildered.

'Nope, that was Plan A. But now that you owe me one, let's team up.' Colin proposed.

'Team up how?' Morty was feeling a bit anxious.

'I'll cover this up, you'll keep your job. And in return, you slip my info to the funeral director. And if they need a celebrant, that's me - win-win.' Colin explained.

'Now I gotta run, dentist's waiting.'

Morty was left speechless as Colin sauntered off.

'See you later, Morty! Your name fits your job. Great doing business with you!' Colin waved, leaving Morty standing there, baffled.

Colin found himself in a queue at the NHS dentist's office. He was surrounded by older people who, ironically, seemed to have tooth problems despite many of them not having any teeth. He mused about how the younger generation tended to go to private dentists, but he was here for now, unable to afford private care.

'Next!' called out the receptionist.
'Hi, I have an appointment with Pearly; sorry I'm a tad late, just 15 minutes. But hey, better late than never, right?'

Colin grinned at the receptionist, hoping for some leniency.

She shot him a disdainful look.

'Your name?'
'Colin Bott, with two T's,' he replied.
'Age?'
'53.
'Date of Birth?'
'February 14, 1970.'
'Could you check my details on your system instead of grilling me?'

Colin flashed a charming smile, trying to ease the tension.

The receptionist remained stoic, not responding to Colin's attempt at humour. She passed over a form and a pen.

'Have a seat and someone will call you.'

'Fine, I'll just wait here for Pearly.'

Colin scanned the room looking for a seat and found himself next to an old woman. She was engrossed in her iPhone, seemingly amused by something. Unknown to her, her earphones weren't plugged in, and her YouTube entertainment echoed for everyone in the clinic.

'Hi there.'

Colin greeted the old woman politely.

'What? She glanced at Colin, confused.
'I was saying hi. Looks like you're enjoying your YouTube videos.' Colin tried to speak louder.

'I'm watching funny stuff.' she replied, still oblivious.

'That's what I thought, funny videos.'
Colin almost shouted, trying to be heard over the sound.

'I'm sorry, I have my earphones in, I can't hear a word you're saying, young man.' she said.

Colin noticed her unconnected earphones and swiftly grabbed the cable, plugging it into her phone.

'There you go, that should help you listen better.'

The old woman seemed unfazed, not even acknowledging the change in her audio setup.

The receptionist shot Colin a disapproving look.

'No worries, just helping her enjoy her YouTube better.'

Colin was thinking, 'What a bunch of losers. Hurry up, my tooth is killing me.'

'You deserve to have a toothache because you are not a nice man.' Said the person behind Colin.

Colin spun around. 'Deserve a toothache? That's not very nice, especially coming from a little girl like you. Well, I'm not Mr Nasty, it's just when the toothache kicks in, the pain is drilling a hole in my brain.'

Colin was trying to lighten the mood.

The little girl gazed at him, seemingly sceptical of Colin's claims.

'Is she your grandma?'

Colin pointed towards the old woman beside him.

The little girl stayed silent.

'Ah, the silent treatment, I see. Are you suffering from toothache as well? Too many sweets, and now you're in for it. Granny here, she probably spoiled you, right? Now both of you are facing the consequences.'

Colin teased the little girl.

'Mr. Colin Bott?' called the receptionist.

Colin waved his hand and approached the reception desk.

'Pearly, your dentist, left about 10 minutes ago. You were late and she has a personal appointment. We've rescheduled your appointment for two weeks from now. Is that alright with you?'

'So, let me get this straight. I've waited around 20 minutes only to be told my appointment's been axed because I was late?'

Colin raised an eyebrow.

'Well, Mr. Bott, you did walk away from our chat earlier; we didn't finish it, so that's on you, not me.'

'What are you talking about; this is terrible service! What about my toothache? Am I supposed to suffer for another two weeks?'

Colin wasn't happy.

The receptionist handed him a small bag of medicine.

'Here's your prescription. Your dentist left it before she left. It may help in the meantime. Thank you, and have a lovely day.'

Colin was seething; he grabbed his medication and stormed out. As he passed a side door, he noticed a box with client survey forms. Grabbing one, he glanced back at the receptionists, as if to suggest he'd be leaving a scathing review. With that, he left the premises.

'I thought you were going to keep him waiting for another half-hour.' Remarked the second receptionist, seated beside her colleague.

'Well, that was the plan, but he started muttering to himself and having a chat with the air. He seems a bit odd, if you ask me. I didn't want him upsetting any of the other clients here.' They both chuckled.

Colin went to Tesco, and started eyeing the microwavable options for his dinner.

'What's this—vegan spaghetti? Doesn't look too appetizing. And lasagne with basil and fresh tomato? How can it be fresh when it's been sitting here for days? False advertising. Can't trust the packaging, not to mention the price they're asking for these things. They call it convenience food, but really...'

'Are you looking for a bargain and trying to save some cash? If so, I wouldn't bother with that kind of food. My mum always taught me to spend money wisely.'

The words of wisdom were coming from a 7-year-old girl, sounding like she was 25. Colin glanced around, looking for the girl's parents.

'So, it's you again.'

Colin smiled, wondering where the girl's guardian was.

'Alright, show me how to be smart with my money.'

He followed the girl to the reduced items section of the supermarket.

'What am I looking at here?'

'These are the reduced items; they are close to their expiry date or just discounted. You can get cheaper things here that are still good, you know. They used to have hot chicken here, and my mum and I loved it. But we'd come after 6 pm when it was all half-price.'

Colin bent down to inspect the lower shelves. There were plenty of reduced-to-clear items, priced significantly lower in price than the regular products.

'These are great! I've never noticed this before; I'm a bit posh, you know. I don't usually go for the cheaper stuff. Well, thank you very much for your, for your advice.'

Colin said, turning around, only to find the little girl had vanished. He left the supermarket and strolled along the street carrying his bag of groceries. And then he heard the young girl's voice singing

"You are my sunshine, my only sunshine You make me happy when skies are grey

You'll never know dear how much I love you Please don't take my sunshine away."

As he turned around, he spotted the girl seated on a bench inside the bus stop.

'Are you following me? Where are your parents?' Colin inquired.

'Busy,' was the girl's simple reply.

'Well, you should head home. Do you live nearby?' Colin asked.

'Nope.'

'Okay, so you're waiting for a bus then?' Colin tried again.

'Uh uh,' the girl said.

Colin decided to let her be, assuming she was waiting for a bus. As he continued walking toward his flat, the girl started singing again and seemed to be following him.

'What are you doing? Stop following me. There's no bus stop around here for miles,' Colin urged, quickening his pace to avoid her. But the girl seemed remarkably energetic, keeping up effortlessly.

'Thank goodness,' Colin muttered to himself when he looked back and saw no sign of her.

'Hi, it's me again!' The girl appeared out of nowhere, startling Colin.

Next time, you need to wear a pair of running shoes to keep up with me. Remember, I'm younger and quicker,'

Flustered, Colin looked around.

'You're very annoying; go home. You're like those persistent ghosts I can't shake off, always pestering me.'

Suddenly, Colin realized what he'd said, took a deep breath, and muttered.

'Not again!'

But the girl had vanished. Colin hurried toward his flat, just a few steps away.

Once in the flat he locked the door and turned around. He felt secure until he noticed the girl sitting on his sofa, waving at him.

'How did you get in here?'

I don't know, you tell me. It seems wherever you go, I keep seeing you also. So, why am I here?'

Colin placed his groceries in the fridge and sighed, 'I thought I was done with this strange stuff, yet here I am, having a conversation with...whatever you are, inside my house.'

'Did you even bother to ask my name?'

'Okay, let's clear this up. Have a seat, let's talk.' They sat at the kitchen table.

'I'm Leila, and I'm 7 years old.'

'Just call me Colin, and please don't ask my age. Can you explain why you're always with me?

'I hope you can tell *me* why I'm always with

you.'

'So, you're suggesting it's my fault that you're here. I don't understand. Can't you just go home? You're not a client of mine for a funeral service. Where did you come from?'

Colin was, puzzled.

'I came from the hospital where you visited this morning.'

Colin started to recall the incident at the hospital when someone touched his hand.

'It was you? You held my hand.'

'Yeah, I felt cold and alone, and then I saw you. Since then, I've been following you. I tried talking to others, but nobody heard me or saw me except you.'

Colin stared at Leila, thinking about his next move.

'I think someone will call me to perform your funeral service. That's why you're here.'

The girl's eyes widened.

'You mean I'm dead?'

'I suppose so. Otherwise, I wouldn't be talking to you and you wouldn't have appeared out of thin air. Yes, I think you're dead.'

Colin hesitantly spoke. Realising the impact of his words, he tried to console Leila.

'I'm sorry I said that, but it's the only explanation for all this.'

He handed the little girl a roll of toilet tissue to dry her tears. In that instant, Colin sensed a strange energy as Leila took the tissue and wiped her face.

'Wait, can you do it again?' Colin asked.

'Do what?' Leila looked puzzled.

'That thing, grab another tissue and wipe your face or nose, please.' Colin urged.

Still uncertain, Leila followed his request, taking another tissue and blowing her nose.

'How did you do that? I mean, how can you touch things? They never do that; they can't touch things. That's why they always ask for my help.'

Colin exclaimed.

'I don't understand what you mean, Colin, but I'm not feeling well. I feel strange.'

Suddenly, the little girl began to slowly vanish.

'Wait! Let's talk more, Leila!'

Colin called out, but she faded away.

The next day brought another funeral assignment for Colin.

As he finished up the service at the crematorium, he noticed that only a handful of people attended, all appearing rather destitute. One of the attendees was an elderly lady being pushed in a wheelchair by a carer. Approaching her, Colin gently asked.

'Did you enjoy the service? It's for your husband's funeral, right?'

The elderly lady, suffering from dementia and hearing difficulties, couldn't quite understand which funeral she was attending.

Colin discreetly slipped his business card into the lady's hand and whispered, 'maybe you'd like to call me sometime.'

There was no response from the old woman. As the carer wheeled the chair away from Colin, the elderly lady, unnoticed by the carer, gave Colin the finger. Colin. He couldn't help but smile at the unexpected reaction.

'Isn't she sweet?' came the cynical remark from Kevin who was standing behind Colin.

'Hi, Kev! I didn't realize you were here. How's work, busy as usual?'

'Nah, pretty much the same every day.'

'Really? I wish I could say the same. Work is still slow for me, Kevin, unfortunately.'

'Don't worry, Colin. You'll be fine. Hey, do you see those two guys coming our way?

Kevin pointed towards the approaching figures.

'Are they from the funeral service?'

Colin asked.

'Yes, they own three funeral branches in town. It's a family business, Crocs & Matt Funeral Services. This is your chance to introduce yourself, Colin. Go ahead.'

Colin walked over to the two men.

'Hi there, good morning.'

He greeted them casually; he didn't want to make it obvious that he had an agenda.

'Morning'

The two men replied simultaneously.
Colin continued.

'Are you conducting the next service? There seems to be quite a gathering.'

'Are you attending the funeral?' one of the men asked.

'No, I just finished a service in the small chapel. I'm a funeral celebrant. I'm Colin Bott at your service.'

He handed over his business card and brochures.

'If you'd like more information about me and how to contact me. Everything you need is there.'

'Hmm, yes, I see. Seems like you know your business, Colin.'

One of the men remarked, whispering to his

colleague.

'Eh, my colleague here thinks maybe we should try your service. What do you think?'

Colin felt excited at the prospect of a new contact.

'Well, just let me know. I'm sure I can fit you into my busy schedule.' he replied enthusiastically.

'As a matter of fact, we have a new funeral in the pipeline. Maybe you can handle that for us.'

'Of course, I'd be glad to. When is the funeral?'

'I'll send you the details today. You have your email and contacts here, right?' the other man interjected.

'Yes, everything is there. Well, except my fee and bank account details. I can provide those when I email you and once the services are completed.'

The two men exchanged glances, raised their eyebrows, and cleared their throats.

'You see, Colin, the service is for an unborn baby, and we don't usually charge the parents or family.' the man clarified.

'Free? Like a charity?' Colin asked, taken aback.

'Yes, like a charity. But it's a win-win situation, right? It's the first time we'll be working together, and you'll be doing good for the family. Who knows, more jobs might come your way.' the man explained optimistically.

Colin was a bit disappointed; a free job wasn't what he needed at the moment, but he considered the potential for future business.

'Not a problem, I'd be happy to help.'
He said, although not entirely convinced.

'Okay, it's settled then. See you around, Colin. We have a funeral to attend. Thanks again.

The men walked off leaving Colin a bit uncertain about the turn of events.
Approaching the car park, he spotted Leila seated on a bench, a smile directed at him.
Leila gestured towards the two men Colin had been talking to.

'Who were they?'
Colin chuckled.
'Ah, those two? They're my new potential business partners. Scratch that, not potential anymore, we're practically best buds now. They handed me a job, not exactly what I expected, but it's a start.'

Leila raised an eyebrow.

'They're recruiting you to be one of the Men in Black?'
Colin looked puzzled.
'Men in Black?'
'Like from the movies, hunting aliens

chasing aliens and saving the world!'

Colin laughed.

'Leila, they're not from the Men in Black movie. They're Funeral Directors. They're the people who give me work. If I get work, I pay bills, get groceries, feed Lucifer.' He nodded toward a cat lounging nearby.

'Do you understand the kind of job I have now?'

'I still think they just want to suck up to you. I don't like them.'

Colin grinned.

'Well, maybe you're onto something there, but I've got nothing to lose. Gotta grab opportunities while they're around, right?

Anway, what brings you here? Are you attending a funeral? Is someone's service taking place?'

'I'm here to see you. I don't know anything about the service. Is it the one you've been working at inside the church, talking about the old grandpa?' Leila replied.

'What? Wait, were you inside the chapel? And how did you know the deceased is an old man? His coffin was completely closed.'

Colin was a bit bemused.

'I saw him standing beside you. Didn't you see him?' Leila asked.

'No, that part I still don't understand.

Not every corpse wants to communicate or request something from me. Sometimes it's more straightforward, believe me, I prefer it that way. Less work, less stress. No offense, but you're not my client yet, and I'm not entirely sure why you're here talking to me. Also, let me correct you, it's not a church; it's a chapel—a crematorium chapel where services for the departed are conducted. Anyway, let's change the topic. I don't want to upset you.'

Colin settled beside Leila.

'Please help me find my dad. I want to know who he is and tell him to take care of my mum. She needs help. You mentioned I'm already gone, and I feel sorry for my mum; she'll be alone.'

Leila expressed her intense sadness to Colin.

'I truly wish I could assist, but I'm not sure where to start. Do you want me to speak with your mum? Perhaps that could be a beginning.'

He noticed Leila's unhappiness, and she nodded.

They sat together inside the car.

'You know, the good thing about you being a ghost is that you can walk through walls. You don't need to drive a car; you just pop out and be wherever you want to be. I wish I could do that.'

Colin mused.

'So, you want to be dead, too?'

'Nah, not yet. I've got so much on my bucket

list.'

Colin attempted to start the car.

'This engine has been troublesome all morning.'

The car wouldn't start, and he kept trying.

'Bloody Hell, don't die on me, You .....'

Colin muttered, glancing at Leila, and trying not to swear in front of her.

'The bonnet of the car suddenly popped open and then slammed shut again.
'Did you do that?'

Colin widened his eyes, and looked at Leila.

'Yeah, I did. My mom's boyfriend used to do that whenever his car didn't start. Come on, try it again.' Leila encouraged.
Colin tried again, and this time, the engine burst into life. As they drove along, Colin noticed Leila quietly observing their surroundings.

'Where are we heading? Where does your mum live?'
'She's in the hospital. That's the last place I saw her, and she was crying.'

Shortly after, the car engine abruptly stopped and wouldn't start.
'Come on, for the love of God.'

Leila tried her trick again, opening and banging the bonnet repeatedly.

'Stop, Leila! My car is too old to take that kind of treatment. You're trying to destroy it, not fix it. Let it be. Let's wait to see if we can call a mechanic or maybe a taxi if there's signal around here.'

They were walking along a country road and Colin kept checking his phone for a signal.

'Look, Colin, there's a swan over there!'

Leila exclaimed, amused by the swan in a pond near the side of the road.

Leila ran towards the pond.

'Hey, Leila, be careful. You're already... you know.' Colin cautioned.

'Look, Colin, there's another one! Oh, and there's a little one.' Leila excitedly pointed out.

Colin and Leila sat under a large tree and watched the swan family.

'You can see they're a family, Leila. That one's the dad, the slightly smaller one's the mom, and the little one is their child.'

Talking with Leila made Colin feel happy, despite her not being his own daughter. Leila's striking features and engaging personality made their conversations delightful.

He watched Leila's having fun as she played

by the loch, tossing stones while singing her familiar tune.

> *"You are my sunshine, my only sunshine*
> *You make me happy when skies are grey*
> *You'll never know, dear, how much I love you*
> *Please don't take my sunshine away"*

He approached Leila and sat beside her.

'What's the last memory you have of being with your mom, Leila?'
'Huh?'
She turned her head.
'I'm not sure. I see myself and my mum in the car. She was upset, crying, I think she was talking with her boyfriend. There was a truck next to us, the man was yelling at my mum; then there was a loud noise from his truck. My mum drove faster, and the truck was making a noise again and then... I don't know what happened. I felt nothing. I saw my mom outside the car, crying, trying to stop other cars. She was waving, and nobody wanted to help her. Then there were lots of flashing blue lights and different voices. The next thing I remember is being in the hospital, and then I saw you. So, I followed you to that dark place. It was so cold, I was scared, so I held your hand.'

Colin struggled to take in all the information Leila had just shared with him. It was clear that she had been in an accident with her mum.

Suddenly, text messages started flooding

Colin's phone, it was finally catching a signal. He paced back and forth, angling his phone upward, attempting to improve the connection and make a call.

'Hello, is this the Fancy Taxi company? Hi, we need a taxi at the loch just near the crematorium, about 10 minutes away. How soon can you get here? Alright, we'll wait. Just me and my daughter. Thank you.'

He just realised that Leila was not a person. 'Shit, why did I say that?'

Leila had gone back to gleefully tossing stones into the loch. Observing her, he pondered how different she seemed from the other deceased he'd encountered. There was an inexplicable liveliness about her, as if she were still alive. Perhaps it was her youth, her angelic face that reminded him of someone he once knew. He could vividly hear her laughter, visualising a young girl playing in a playground in Cornwall. He made up his mind to go back and visit her sometime.

'Leila, the taxi will be here any minute. Can you please stop that? I don't want to startle the driver.'

But Leila, like any typical child, paid no heed to his words.

'Colin, look over there! Seems like there's a party happening, and someone's waving at us. Well, maybe just at you.' Leila exclaimed.

Colin glanced toward the far end of the loch, noticing a commotion with blue lights and a gathering of people.

'I'm not sure if that woman is waving at us. I think there might be an accident; it's not a party, Leila. Great, the taxi is here.'

Leila and Colin sat side by side in the taxi, and Leila noticed a small decorative figure hanging from the driver's mirror—an unmistakable Catholic cross and a miniature house, labelled - 'Forever Home.'

'Where are we headed?' said the taxi driver.

'Tell him Forever Home,' said Leila.

'What? I thought we were going to the hospital.'

The taxi driver was surprised at what Colin was saying.

'I didn't say I'm taking you to the hospital. I asked where we're headed.'

'Oh, I'm sorry. Just take us to Forever Home,' said Colin.

'I was told I'd be picking up two passengers.'

'Ah, yes, I forgot. My daughter was picked up by her mother earlier, so it's just me. Apologies for the confusion.'

Feeling a bit uneasy, the driver switched on the radio news, and a report about a body found in the nearby loch caught their attention.

'So, that's why we—I mean, I saw a crowd and blue lights across the loch. Thought it might be an accident. I'd bet it was a woman,' said Colin.

The taxi drivers throat visibly tightened as he listened to the one side of their conversation.

'How did you know it was a woman? It's not confirmed yet.' he stammered nervously.

Colin, unaware of the driver's discomfort, continued.

'Well, that's usually the case, right? Men dump their wives or girlfriends' bodies in secluded spots so no one can find them. I imagine she's a middle-aged brunette with long hair.'

Colin was describing the woman they had seen waving at them earlier.

'Hmm, I wonder if I'll get to organize her funeral.' he mused casually.

The taxi driver, was by now visibly anxious. he pressed harder on the accelerator, eager to get to their destination.

Suddenly, he locked the plastic see through divider and flashed a nervous smile at Colin.

'Safety first.' he stammered again.

Colin couldn't resist and quipped.

'Is that for our safety or yours?'

The driver didn't answer, still feeling

anxious and a bit nervous. He kept looking at Colin in his mirror until they arrived at their destination.

> 'That'll be £20.50. How'll you be paying?' the driver asked.
> 'Card or cash?' Colin inquired.
> 'I take both, as long as you're the one paying.'

The driver quipped, sliding the card machine towards Colin through the small window in the divider.

'Could you charge £20 on the card and I'll give you the rest in cash, plus a tip? I'm meticulous about keeping my bank account neat.'

Colin was slightly embarrassed; he knew he didn't have enough money in the bank.

The taxi driver adjusted the card machine to exactly £20.

'Here you go, £20.' he confirmed.

Colin tapped his card and handed over a pound to the driver.

'Keep the change, thank you,' said Colin stepping out of the taxi.

The taxi driver put his foot to the floor and sped off down the road.

'Grumpy old git didn't even say thanks for the tip.' Colin muttered.

He glanced at the building labelled "Forever Home, a Care Facility for the Elderly".

'What in the world are we doing here, Leila?'

Leila didn't respond and walked directly inside, with Colin reluctantly trailing behind her. There were two receptionists engrossed in a conversation about their favourite TV show, Coronation Street. They didn't notice Colin's arrival as he followed Leila through the corridors. She seemed uncertain of where she was going, but she seemed to have a strange sense of familiarity, which prompted her to venture further into the care home.

'Psst, Leila, wait! What's going on? We shouldn't be here.' Colin whispered urgently.

Leila walked on.

'Oi, you stubborn kid; you never listen to me.' Colin grumbled in frustration.

Leila paused at room 101. The door was open and an elderly man was sitting inside in a wheelchair. He was struggling to breathe with a mask on leading to an oxygen tank. He was chuckling at a comedy show on television. Leila stood there, captivated by him, sensing a curious familiarity.

'Oh, there you are! Come on in, don't just stand there.'

The old man called out, switching off the TV, adjusting his wheelchair, and gesturing to the chair beside him.

'Are you speaking to me?' questioned Colin, glancing around while standing behind Leila. He was unsure if the old man was addressing him or if he was aware of Leila's presence. Colin decided it was safer to enter the room, just in case any staff passed by.

The old man pointed at Colin and indicated the chair, inviting him to sit down.

'Hello, I'm Colin Bott. I apologize for interrupting your show. To be honest, I'm not even sure where I am.'

'Don't we all? We're all a bit lost. Every day I wake up asking, "Where am I?" Hahaha!'

The old man chuckled, interrupted by a cough.

'Are you all right?' Colin asked, concerned.

'Do you think I'm all right, young lad? I'm just a few steps from the grave, as you can see.'

'I'm sorry, I didn't mean any offense.'

'It's fine. I enjoy a good joke now and then.'

The old man reassured him.

Colin began to feel a fondness for this elderly man.

'So, Colin, what's your profession?'

'I'm a Funeral Celebrant. I officiate at

funerals...'

Colin started, but the old man interrupted him with a dismissive wave of his hand.

'Okay, okay, I know what a celebrant does. I've been stuck in this place for over a decade. My son tossed me aside after my wife passed. They claimed I've got mild dementia. It wasn't my choice to be here, but hey, as long as my son pays, they treat me like royalty. Anyway, I've been to a few funerals of my old pals here. Seen your type before, talking about the deceased and their lives.'

'Well, it's not just negative things I mention in their eulogies. Some of them had fascinating lives, you know. I suppose you might have had an incredible life before you arrived here too, I imagine.'

'Hmm, you might be onto something, young man. I suppose I had a meaningful life before this. I wish I could remember all of it; but sometimes this mind of mine plays tricks. I don't want to label it as dementia. It's just a part of growing old.'

'You seem content here, though. Your own room, a TV, a private bathroom—what more could you ask for? Seems like you're living your best life.' Colin remarked.

The old man appeared to disagree with Colin's assessment.

'Or perhaps not.' Colin added uneasily.

'Oh, I used to like this place. Nurses were top-notch, carers galore, and all slim and lively 6 to 10 years back. But now? Hell no! Have you noticed those reception witches? Always chit-chatting about their TV shows, ignoring me every time I ring them on the intercom. It takes ages for them to send help when I need to use the loo! Many a time, I've had accidents—both a little sprinkle and the whole shebang, if you catch my drift.

Lazy bunch! I've told my son to ship me off to one of those retirement hotels like the Holiday Inn. A mate of mine's living there; says it's pure luxury! Great grub, fresh sheets and pillows daily, a casino, a pool, and they've even got a pub inside the place.'

'Really? I've never heard about such places. I'd love to have something like that when I retire. No way I'd want to end up in a care home.' remarked Colin.

The old man nodded in agreement.

'Yeah, that's exactly what I've been telling my son—to take me there, just like my pal David. Probably romancing prostitutes every night, ha-ha.'

They shared a laugh.

Suddenly, the old man fell silent, gazing at the wall. Colin noticed and waved his hand in front of the old man's face.

'Is anybody in there? Calling planet Earth! Looks like your battery's running low. By the way, I missed your name.' Colin asked.

'His name is Martin. Leila promptly responded.

'He's, my grandad. Wake him up, Colin.'

'How am I supposed to wake him up? He's not even asleep. Can't you see? His eyes aren't even closed.

'Tell him Norma Jean is here.' Leila insisted.

'What? Who? What are you talking about, Leila? Who is Norma Jean?'

'That's what he calls my mum, Norma Jean.'

'So, your mum's named after Marilyn Monroe?'

'Who's Marilyn Monroe? I said Norma Jean.'

'Well, that's Marilyn Monroe's real name—Norma Jean. You're too young for those things. And really, your mum's name is Norma Jean?'

Colin asked, surprised.

'No, my mum is Sarah. But my grandad here calls her Norma Jean.'

'That's her.' Leila pointed at Sarah's picture in a silver frame on the old man's bedside table. Colin walked over, took the picture, and examined it.

'So, this your mom? I think I've seen her before. '

'Yeah, she's pretty, isn't she?'

'Yeah, I get why your grandad calls her Norma Jean. She looks like Marilyn Monroe, the actress. You probably don't know her, it's before your time. But how is this old man your grandad when your mother looks like Marilyn Monroe?'

'I know this place; it's my mum's workplace. She helps out here, serves meals, and tidies beds. I used to wait for her after she finished her work. I remember when there was a party. Lots of grandpas and grandmas giving me money and gifts. They wanted me to dance and sing on the table. I also remember my mom wearing that dress from the picture, singing for all the grandpas and grandmas.' Leila reminisced.

Colin presumed that the picture of Leila's mom was taken at a Christmas party.

Suddenly, the old man regained consciousness.

'What? Where's Norma Jean? Is she here?' he exclaimed, scanning the room.

'Tell me, did she return? Where is she?'

Colin felt sympathy for the old man.

'It's alright, just relax. Norma Jean is here; she'll be back. She went to get your medicine. Don't worry, just relax. I think you should rest.'

'That's the picture of Norma Jean. She's the one who takes care of me here, always ensuring I'm well and happy. She can sing too, what a lovely voice. That's where my granddaughter Leila gets her beautiful voice from, her mother. My son fell in love with her— who wouldn't? She's a kind person. But that witch woman interfered.'

'What witch woman?' Colin inquired.

'That wife of my son, forgot her name, and I don't want to remember it. She wasn't a good wife. My son wanted to divorce her, but she wouldn't sign the papers. Then Norma Jean and Leila stopped visiting me. I waited every day, Matthew always lied to me, saying they'd come back, but they didn't. So, don't lie to me like Matthew did, saying Norma Jean will come back.'

The old man said, suddenly wiping his tears away.

Colin was helping Martin settle into bed when a voice startled him from behind.

'Excuse me, who are you?'

The stern tone came from a rather imposing woman standing in the doorway, eyeing Colin expectantly.

Colin turned around, trying to sound casual.

'Oh, I'm a friend of Martin's son. Just dropped by for a quick visit.'

'Hmm, I don't recognize you. My name's Doris, and I'm the assistant manager here. I've been here for the past three years, and the only visitor Martin has is his son, Matthew Glenn. And how did you bypass the reception?' Doris asked suspiciously.

'How would you notice,' said Martin. You're

THE CELEBRANT

always engrossed in your favorite TV programme. You're so deep in it, you wouldn't even notice if we escaped this 'prison' of yours. Probably wouldn't even notice if the building were on fire.' Martin added.

'Not now, Martin, don't start with your grumpiness. We always strive to cater to your needs.'

'Cater to my needs; that's a joke! You won't even let me ring up my mate David. I want to check if he's enjoying his spot in paradise. You just want me stuck here till I kick the bucket, in this stinky old place.'

'Okay, now, that's enough Martin,' Doris cautioned.

'Why're you stopping him from talking to his pal?' asked Colin

'Because, his buddy's been gone for a good two years now. Probably living it up in his own version of paradise; just not the one Martin has in mind. Alright, tidy yourself up; your son's dropping by for a visit.' Doris announced.

Colin suddenly panicked.

'You mean Matthew Glenn?'
'Yeah, your *friend* as you put it,' said Doris.
'Yeah, that's great! I'll be absolutely thrilled to see him.'

Colin exaggerated, trying to go along with

the situation.

As Doris dashed off to fetch towels and warm water for Martin's nightly wash, Colin leaned in and whispered.

'Gotta dash. Here is my business card, who knows? Maybe you'll be needing my services one day, Martin. It was great chatting with you. Bye!'

Colin hustled out the door of the care home, Leila trailing behind and calling out to him.

'Where are we going? I thought we were finding my dad, maybe that Matthew guy could be him.'

'First things first, I don't fancy getting into trouble. I'm not keen on being seen by someone who might mistake me for an intruder in their dying father's room.'

'At the right moment, I'll introduce myself as a celebrant. There's a perfect time and place for these sorts of talks. I'm hoping he'll ring me up soon; that's why I left my card with Martin. Anyhow, you're the one who's landed me in this awkward spot. Maybe tomorrow we'll swing by the hospital to visit your mum, is that a deal?'

Leila vanished into thin air again.

'Oh, here we go again, you little rascal, trying to run away from me. This conversation isn't finished.'

As Colin was leaving the care home a couple of residents were coming in being helped by their carers. One of the old ladies looked at Colin talking to Leila, or to himself as it appeared. She remarked to her friend, 'that young lad seems too young to have dementia, don't you think?

'Yeah, dementia is hitting at an early age now. Worrisome, isn't it? At least that's not happening to us. Are we in the pub? I can't see the bar.'

The following day brought another successful job for Colin; it was to be a brief service, and he was early at the crematorium. He wasn't in a rush, feeling satisfied as he watched the service before his, arriving. There was a grand procession led by a piper in full highland dress, the Funeral Director behind, and a long line of family and friends following the hearse.

Colin couldn't help but feel envious. He wished he could conduct a funeral like that, with hundreds in attendance. It was a daydream he could vividly imagine. Suddenly, he snapped out of it, when he was abruptly interrupted by a voice

'Guess who's leading this grand service?'

It was Falker, the Irish celebrant whom Colin didn't particularly like, grinning proudly beside him.

'Oh, didn't see you there, Falker.'
'I'm handling this major service. There might even be some celebrities attending. The deceased was a prominent singer and TV personality who

dropped dead recently, causing quite the social media frenzy. The family chose me for the gig; they wanted the best, naturally.'

'Of course, I bet you'll have a crowd of 200 to 300 people hanging on every word of your eulogy,' said Colin sarcastically, with a smirk on his face.

'I'm at the top, man. I believe some very prominent people in business, politics and the media will attend, so it's significant exposure for me. Next thing you know, I'll be featured on the front-page news tomorrow—"the best celebrant in town" Wish me luck, Colin. Nice chatting with you.'

'Absolutely, Falker! See you around!'

Colin called out, unable to hide his amusement at their brief exchange. He noted the size of the coffin in the hearse, it was huge.

'Hey, tell the funeral director you'll need six strong lads to carry that coffin.'

'Leila spoke, 'I don't like him.'

'Oh, look who's here once more. I thought you were mad at me.'

Leila remained silent; her gaze fixed on Falker.

'Oh, you mean that guy?'

'Yeah, he looks like an ugly dwarf to me.'

'I can understand that, Leila. I feel the same way, and that dwarf, is my nemesis.'

'What's a nemesis?' Leila asked, feeling confused.'

'Never mind, forget I said it. Let's go find your mum.'

As they walked towards the car park, a middle-aged man passed them, catching Leila's attention. She seemed to recognize him—the scent of his cologne, his physique—something about him struck a chord, leaving her unable to explain why. She stopped walking, fixated on the man as he headed towards the chapel.

'Hey, come on. I don't want to lose you again, Leila.' Colin urged.

'That's him.'

Leila pointed to the passing man.

'Who, what, where? What are you talking about, Leila?'

'I found my dad. That's him, in the black jacket, just like the Men in Black.

'Where? I can't see him. Almost everyone's in a black suit.'

Colin scanned the crowd.

'I know it's my dad, Colin. I remember his nice smell,' Leila insisted.

Colin raised an eyebrow.

'You can't just pick anyone and claim they're your dad because of a scent. I could wear your dad's aftershave, and you'd say I'm him. Come on, kiddo.'

He chuckled, sceptical of Leila's claim.

Leila looked crestfallen, unsure of what to say, as memories of her dad were hazy.

'Okay, okay, let's try to find him. What did the staff at the care home say his name was? It was Matthew, wasn't it?'

'Matthew Glenn!' Leila exclaimed.

'Yeah, Matthew Glenn. But how are we going to find him? There's a hundred Men in Black here.'

'I know what to do! Let's go to customer service and have them announce my dad's name.'

Leila suggested.

Colin burst out laughing.

'Leila, this isn't a mall or a grocery store. It's a crematorium. You can't announce a missing person during a funeral service.'

'So, what now?' Leila asked.

'I hate to say this, but we wait. With this huge crowd, we'll be here for a while. Especially with Falker conducting the service, he'll make sure to get attention from all these people here.' Colin sighed.

As he turned around, Leila was nowhere to be seen, leaving him talking to himself.

'Great. I knew you wouldn't listen.' he muttered under his breath.

He made his way toward the chapel, navigating through the crowd that had gathered, just ten minutes before the service was scheduled to start.

'Excuse me, excuse me.'

Colin called out, half-expecting to find a little ghost among the throng of people. He resorted to whispering Leila's name.'

'Leila... psst... Leila.'

Continuing his search, Colin spotted Leila standing next to a tall man engaged in conversation with a group.

'Leila! Don't!'

Colin exclaimed, rushing toward them.

It was too late. Leila had slyly placed her hand on the tall man's.

'Leila! Don't do that!'

But the man, feeling the touch on his hand, glanced around nervously. Colin was at a loss for words, unsure how to approach Leila's dad.

'Uh, err, hi.'

Colin stammered, shifting his feet awkwardly in front of Matthew Glen.

'Hi there. Are you a friend or relative of Rico's?' Matthew asked.

'Who's Rico?'

'The person in the coffin.' replied Matthew.

'Oh, that person! Rico, right. Nope, I mean, I'm not a relative or a friend. But I do know that big guy inside the coffin. I've seen him in a commercial on TV, the one singing Go Compare. I know him intimately... I mean, not that intimately, just, you know, in passing.'

Colin stumbled over his words, making a mess of the situation. Matthew looked thoroughly mystified.

'Yeah, Rico's one of our talents. My company did that commercial you mentioned. So, it's no surprise there are a lot of people paying their respects. That commercial made him famous, I guess.' Matthew explained.

'Oh, so you're the advertising boss I've heard about. Sorry, I didn't catch your name.'

Colin pretended not to know Matthew, just to be sure he was speaking to the right person.

'Apologies, I'm Matthew Glen from Daily News Media. And you are?'

'I'm Colin Bott, a celebrant. And before you ask, no, I'm not doing the service today. That lucky Irish Falker got the job. Well, maybe next time. Maybe if someone you know is almost dying, he he, just kidding.'

Colin attempted to lighten the conversation.

Suddenly, it dawned on Colin that he had given his business card to the old man at the care home, and this man in front of him was his son, Matthew. He noticed Matthew smiling at him.

'Damn it!' Colin cursed inwardly.

'You're the guy who visited my dad yesterday, right? At the care home?'

'Me? Yesterday? Let me think... Where was I yesterday? Oh, right, yeah, I was at the care home, visiting my friend. I mean, my friend's friend. I forgot his name, but maybe I bumped into your dad.'

Colin clumsily tried to cover his tracks.

'I didn't mean anything I said to him. My apologies. Your dad is great, still in good shape, with a good sense of good humour. I'm sure he will live a lot longer.'

Colin was feeling a bit embarrassed.

'It's okay, no worries. I understand what you meant. I accept the fact that my dad is just waiting for the right time to rest. I'm just curious; when you were there yesterday, did you happen to have a child with you?' Matthew inquired.

'Huh, what do you mean, a child?' Colin asked, puzzled.

'It's just that my dad mentioned a little girl visiting him yesterday. He said that she looked like her mother, as if my dad knows the mother of the little girl. Sorry, it's a bit confusing. I'm just wondering. My dad tends to have moments when he talks about his past or anything under the sun. He's suffering from dementia. Hold on, just forget what I've said. The service is about to begin. Well, nice talking to you, Colin.'

Colin gathered his thoughts, pondering whether the old man had seen Leila.

'Wait! ahh, I don't know how to put this. You mentioned your dad sometimes has bouts of dementia?' Colin probed.

'Yeah, unfortunately.'

Colin noticed Leila standing nearby, signalling for him to disclose their location.

Colin swiftly fabricated a story.

'I think he was a bit confused yesterday, talking about the picture of Marilyn Monroe on his side table. Do you have any idea who that person might be? I was convinced it was actually Marilyn Monroe. Then, when I looked closely, she resembled someone I met at the hospital last week.' Colin explained.

'He mentioned the name, Sarah.'

Matthew's face lit up upon hearing someone mention his former partner.

'You mean Sarah Turner?' asked Matthew.

'Yeah, Sarah Turner who looks like Marilyn Monroe. And she worked at the care home before I think..?' Colin said nervously.

'Is she okay? What happened? Why was she

in the hospital?' asked Matthew.

'Well, I didn't know her too well, but she looked like the woman on your dad's side table. I'm quite certain that's her. I'm not sure why she's there. Maybe you can still catch her. Do you want to see her?'

'Yeah, of course! I've been searching for them for years now. Yeah, you could be right maybe she's working there, she used to work at the care home where my dad is, that's where I met her. She just walked away from me without saying goodbye. I don't know what had happened, Anyway, you've given me good news. Which hospital?' He asked.

'Queen Margaret.' Colin replied.

'Thank you, Colin, I will just inform Rico's family that I can't attend the service because something came up.'

Matthew simply waved his hand, signalling a goodbye gesture.

'I'm afraid this won't turn out to be good news.' Colin mumbled, concerned that Matthew might discover the accident involving Leila and Sarah.

Leila stood beside Colin, watching her dad walk away. That was all she wanted - for her mum not to be alone without her.

'Are you happy now, Leila?' Colin asked.

'I always knew my dad didn't leave us. He did look for us.'

'Yes, he did, Leila. He did.'

As the bagpipes began to play and people started to gather in line toward the chapel, the funeral service for Rico, the celebrity, was about to begin.

Colin felt sympathy for Leila. Watching her enjoy the warm sun and the fresh air, Colin softly muttered,

'Rest in peace, Leila'

His phone rang and he answered he answered.

'Hello, Colin Bott speaking.'

'Hi, it's Morty, your buddy from the morgue at the hospital.'

'Ah, Morty! Of course, I remember our incident in the mortuary. You wouldn't believe where I am right now—I'm at a funeral for that chap, the hefty one we teased a bit at when we were trying to get him up off the floor.

So, what can I do for you?'

Morty explained, 'I've got a task for you. My supervisor wants me to arrange for the pickup of that body you saw that's been unclaimed for about two months; the one from the car accident. Unfortunately, no family has come forward, so we need to take care of it. The council will cover a modest funeral with a few friends. You're the first person I thought of for this. I'll pass on your details to the funeral director so you can handle the service.

Morty sounded pleased to involve Colin.

'That's great, Morty. I owe you one.'

'Hey, Colin, I'm not finished yet. It's not just one job—I have two for you. I'm awaiting instructions at the office. I'm expecting the body of a little girl, the daughter of the woman. It's a tragic case; both mother and daughter lost their lives in a car accident caused by a reckless truck driver trying to overtake. Despicable.'

Morty elaborated.

Colin's demeanour suddenly shifted to nervousness.

'Morty, what's the mother's name?'

'Let me check the records... Here it is. Sarah Turner, deceased. The daughter in the ICU is Leila Turner, just seven years old. The doctors are considering ending he life support.'

Colin felt like he might faint, his head spinning, and his balance wavering. He couldn't believe what he was hearing.

He recollected the anxious woman at the hospital reception. The memory of the other body at the morgue lingered, Morty's warning vivid in his mind not to look at it. However, he couldn't help but notice the name tag, identifying her as Susan Turner. Leila's harrowing account of the car accident, where her mother had waved for assistance, resurfaced in his thoughts.

Suddenly, Carmen's words came back in Colin's mind:

'Okay, so ghosts or spirits have three different stages. The third stage is when they can stroll, visit loved ones, and cause some spooky activities. But when it's time for them to transition, they become apparitions. These folks are in a waiting zone, not quite dead but waiting for whatever comes next.'

'Like being in a coma?' Colin suggested.
'Similar idea.' Carmen agreed.

'Colin, are you still there?'
 Morty's voice echoed through the phone.
Colin turned around and caught sight of Leila. There was an ethereal glow about her, a radiance he hadn't witnessed before. She seemed on the brink of transcending into another realm, slowly fading into the air.

'Colin, something's happening to me. I feel so cold... help me!' Leila cried out desperately.
'Leila, hold on!'

Colin rushed toward her, but she was slipping away. Panic surged through him, thoughts racing. He had to make a decision, and fast. Leila wasn't gone yet; perhaps there was still a chance to save her, or at least give her a moment to see her father, Matthew, before the doctors made a final decision on her life support.

'Morty what time did you mention the doctors were going to disconnect Leila?'
'Well, in about 20 minutes. Why?'
'Damn it!'

Colin exclaimed, scanning for someone to assist him. Without a car, he needed help getting to the hospital.

Then, he spotted Matthew still in the parking lot, engaged in conversation and preparing to head to his car. In that instant, Colin made a critical choice—he had to disclose the truth about Matthew's family, about Sarah and Leila. Matthew needed to know he was running out of time to see his daughter alive.

'Matthew!... Matthew!'

Colin frantically waved his hands, knowing it was unlikely Matthew would notice him from where he was. He hesitated, glancing at his polished shoes.

'Oh, to hell with it.' he muttered.

He sprinted across the muddy grass and the flower beds, waving and shouting at Matthew. He had to reach the lower part of the hill where Matthew was parked.

He managed to flag down Matthew's car, by standing in the middle of the road arms outstretched. Startled, Matthew slammed on the brakes, completely bewildered by Colin's sudden appearance.

'What on earth are you doing Colin?'
'I need to go with you to the hospital. I'll

explain everything later, but time's running out, please.' Colin was gasping for breath.

'Get in, you nearly got yourself killed running in front of the car, Colin, not smart.'

Colin, unapologetic for his actions, remained silent, contemplating how to explain the situation to Matthew.

'Matthew, could you drive faster, please? We have to reach the hospital in less than 20 minutes'

Matthew glanced at Colin, concerned.

'What's going on, Colin? Is there something you need to tell me? Is this about Sarah?'

'I'm sorry, Matthew. I'm a bit confused too. I received a call from someone I know at the hospital. Your daughter needs you.'

'What do you mean? Why is my daughter in the hospital? I'm completely lost here, Colin. You mentioned meeting Sarah at the hospital— I thought she worked there. Why are you talking about my daughter, and how do you even know about her?'

'I was at the hospital last week for a check-up, and there was an...' Colin paused, hesitating.

'What, Colin? Spit it out, speak up.' Matthew urged.

'Sarah was in an accident last week along with your daughter. That's why they're both hospitalized.'

'Oh, God, no.' Matthew whispered in shock.

'I'm sorry, Matthew, but Sarah didn't make it. I believe she passed away in the accident.'

'What about my daughter? What about Leila?'

'I don't have all the details, but my friend from the hospital mentioned they're considering removing life support for your daughter. I'm sorry; I only found out about this today.'

Matthew drove faster, even running a red light. Colin, on the brink of a panic attack, frantically searched for his forgotten seatbelt.

Finally, they arrived at Queens Margaret Hospital.

Colin and Matthew ran to the information desk, desperate to locate the ICU room. The staff directed them, and they hurried through the vast hospital. However, they became confused by all the identical corridors and hallways.

Amidst the chaos, Colin was suddenly aware of Sarah. She appeared beside him, and although Mathew couldn't hear or see her, she started to guide them to the ICU unit.

Matthew was frustrated as they seemed to be running in circles, causing him to stop and hold his head in bewilderment; he was on the verge of surrender.

'Matthew, not that way. It's the other hallway, come on, trust me.'

Colin urged desperately.

They eventually spotted a sign indicating the

THE CELEBRANT

ICU direction at the bottom of the east wing. Following it, they arrived at Leila's room, their hands trembling as they prepared to open the door, only to find the doctor opening it from the inside.

'Is my daughter, Leila, still here?'

Matthew's voice trembled with emotion.

'Are you...?' the doctor began.
'Yes, I want to see my daughter, please...'

Matthew's attempt to control his emotions crumbled; tears were streaming down his face.

Colin fought back tears as well, placing a hand over his mouth, wrestling with a sense of guilt. He wished he had listened to Leila earlier when she sought his help to find her dad. It wasn't for herself; she wanted her father to see her mother, Sarah, one last time, for them to reunite.

'If only I had listened to Leila sooner...' Colin's thoughts raced, filled with regret.

The doctor placed a comforting hand on Matthew's shoulder, sensing the father's pain. It was a scene he had witnessed numerous times in his line of work—the anguish and suffering of families. Understanding how to navigate such situations, he aimed to maintain calmness, allowing the family to grieve and eventually regain composure and comprehend the situation.

'It's okay to grieve, but sometimes miracles

happen in mysterious ways. Your daughter has been given a second chance at life. She's stable now, having woken up from her coma. She's sleeping now so let's give her the time she needs to rest,' the doctor explained.

'What? What do you mean?' Matthew's confusion was evident.

'The management and medical team had decided to remove life support, but about 30 minutes ago, she suddenly woke up and was asking for her mother. It seems she fought back for her life. We've tried reaching out to the authorities to locate her family but we couldn't find any. I'm glad you're here, Mr...? the doctor inquired.

'Matthew Glenn.' He shook the doctor's hand.

'And I'm Colin Bott, not a family member, just a friend'

The door to the ICU opened and a nurse came out and spoke to the doctor.

'Doctor, Leila is awake.'

'Go ahead, it's time to see your daughter Mr Glenn'

Colin waited outside the ICU as the doctor walked away, nodding to Colin before pausing, seemingly struck by a thought.

'What was your name again?' the doctor asked.

'Colin Bott.'

'Hmm. I thought I heard Leila calling your

name. Maybe not. Alright, goodbye.'

He looked confused as he left.
'I bet she did.' Colin smiled.

A week later Colin was conducting a graveside service at the City Cemetery. He spoke the eulogy -

'Peter Baskin lived a life filled with kindness, compassion, and warmth. He had a way of making everyone feel valued and loved. His laughter was infectious, bringing joy to those around him. He had a heart that overflowed with generosity and understanding, always ready to lend a helping hand to anyone in need.

Today, we say goodbye to a remarkable individual, but we also celebrate a life well-lived. Let us carry the lessons Peter Baskin taught us and honor him by living our lives with the same compassion and love that he shared with us. So, as we commit Peter Baskins remains to the earth, we say, Ashes to ashes, dust to dust, honoring the journey of his life and recognizing the interconnectedness of all things. His presence will be deeply missed, but his spirit will forever remain in our hearts.'

The funeral service concluded, marking the end of another task for Colin, and a pay day for him. Despite this, he remained somewhat despondent about Leila's situation. It had been two weeks without any updates from Matthew. The mere thought of returning to the hospital brought a sense of reluctance. The last he heard from Morty, was that Matthew had opted for a swift private cremation for Sarah. Additionally, he decided to take his daughter Leila, to Switzerland for her ongoing recovery.

As Colin prepared to start his car, his phone rang.

'Hello, Colin Bott speaking.'

'Hey, Colin, it's Marco. Have you seen today's obituary section in The Daily newspaper?'

'No, I haven't. What's in it, Marco?'

'You never mentioned that you're a star,' chuckled Marco.

'What do you mean?' Colin asked, a bit puzzled.

'Just check it out on their website, The Daily News. I'd love to chat, but customers are flooding in after my renovations. Business is booming again. Catch you later, my friend.'

Marco ended the call.

Colin Googled the newspaper's website. He found the front-page news and scrolled through it, wondering what Marco meant. To his astonishment, he stumbled upon a full-page article featuring his face, mirroring the design of his Celebrant brochure. Underneath, there was a caption that left him surprised and intrigued. It took the form of a testimonial, and an advertisement for Colin's services.

"Mr. Colin Bott is an incredible individual who goes above and beyond to ensure that the ceremony is personal, meaningful, and respectful. I am immensely grateful for his dedication and would highly recommend him to anyone seeking a compassionate and skilled celebrant during their time of need. Five stars doesn't seem enough to truly express our gratitude. From Matthew Glenn – CEO/President of Daily News .uk."

Colin felt overwhelmed with joy upon seeing his face in the Nationwide Newspaper. A free advertisement and a positive review—something he couldn't have afforded, especially a full-page ad. Grinning from ear to ear, he started the car and switched on the radio.

As a familiar song played, memories flooded back, reminding him of moments when Leila used to follow him around.

> *You are my sunshine, my only sunshine*
> *You make me happy when skies are grey*
> *You'll never know, dear, how much I love you*
> *Please don't take my sunshine away*
>
> *The other night, dear, as I laid sleeping*
> *I dreamed I held you in my arms*

When I awoke, dear, I was mistaken
So I hung my head and cried

He drove past the loch where he and Leila once spent time together. He pulled into a layby and stopped the car. He immersed himself in the serene atmosphere, savouring the calmness of the wind and the sound of the loch's waters lapping against the shore. He closed his eyes, and smiled as he recalled Leila's voice.

'You'll always be the best celebrant to me, because you're my best friend.' Her words lingered pleasantly in his mind.

The phone rang, and he answered -
'Hello, Colin Bott, at Your Service.'

AFTERWORD

Colin Bott's story is not yet finished, there will be more, out of this world, story to unveil; more witty and humorous adventures to come. The next adventure will divulge more about Colin's life and the people who surround him. If you enjoyed this book, you will definitely be waiting for the release of the second book of comedy and corpses.

ABOUT THE AUTHOR

A & A Fairweather

This book is the result of the collaboration between Alan Fairweather and Anezia Sanchez.

Alan Fairweather, known as "The Motivation Doctor," is an International Speaker, Author, and Business Development Expert. With a portfolio of 7 published books. He is also recognized as a celebrant and a voice-over narrator.

Anezia Sanchez, the founder of Anezia's Cats and Dogs Shelter, leads a non-profit charity dedicated to aiding abused and abandoned cats and dogs in the Philippines. Beyond her philanthropic efforts, she is a multi-talented individual, engaging in artistry, costume design, and various hobbies. Her artistic creations are available for purchase on different online platforms such as Etsy, eBay, and Pinterest (Anezia Shop), with all proceeds directed towards her charitable cause. In 2023, she published her first book, "LOVE YOU TOO," a romantic novel, with all proceeds dedicated to supporting her charity.

Printed in Great Britain
by Amazon